Endorsements for BRAVE MOM

"Parenthood is the most amazing, rewarding, and terrifying job any of us will ever undertake. In *Brave Mom*, Sherry Surratt has created a safe place for moms to retreat — a place where they can admit that they're afraid, be refreshed and revitalized by Sherry's words of encouragement, and dive confidently back into the trenches of parenthood with the knowledge that they are not alone."

> —MARK BATTERSON, New York Times bestselling
> author of *The Circle Maker*

"Is there anything quite like being a mom that surfaces the deep, unconscious fears that lurk in our souls? The answer is no. And Sherry Surratt plumbs those depths with us. From nasal syringes to expectations to cancer and beyond, this book intersects those fears with Jesus, and as a result, the reader comes out different on the other side."

> —NANCY ORTBERG, author of *Looking for God: An Unexpected
> Journey through Tattoos, Tofu, and Pronouns*

"Moms make the world go round! But too many of them are burdened by the fear that they're not measuring up. We hear stories like this every day at Focus on the Family. Sherry Surratt's book offers time-tested, biblically sound advice for moms in the challenges they face. I highly recommend it."

> —JIM DALY, President, Focus on the Family

"It takes a truly brave mom to admit she'll never be the perfect mother, but she can be just what God planned for her children. Sherry Surratt talks about fears many moms secretly face, and provides clear, straightforward guidance on how to courageously confront those fears. Like she says, 'While you won't be a perfect mom, you already are the perfect mom for your kids.' Read this book and you'll see why."

—REGGIE JOINER, CEO and founder
of Orange Family Ministry

"The overwhelming love we feel for our children is often accompanied by equally overwhelming fear. Sherry Surratt takes us to the heart of those fears, attacking and subduing them with truth and practical new ways to think. Every mom will relate!"

—POLLY LOTT, mother of two, Director of Ministries,
Southeast Christian Church in Parker, Colorado

BRAVE MOM

BRAVE
MOM

FACING AND OVERCOMING
YOUR REAL MOM FEARS

SHERRY SURRATT

President and CEO of MOPS International

ZONDERVAN

Brave Mom

Copyright © 2014 by MOPS International, Inc.

This title is also available as a Zondervan ebook. Visit www.zondervan.com/ebooks.

Requests for information should be addressed to:

Zondervan, 3900 *Sparks Dr. SE, Grand Rapids, Michigan 49530*

Library of Congress Cataloging-in-Publication Data

Surratt, Sherry, 1962-
    Brave mom : facing and overcoming your real mom fears / Sherry Surratt. — 1st [edition].
       pages cm
     ISBN 978-0-310-34037-9 (softcover)
    1. Motherhood — Religious aspects — Christianity. 2. Christian women — Religious life. 3. Fear — Religious aspects — Christianity. I. Title.
BV4529.18.S87 2014
248.8'431 — dc23
                                                2014016661

Cover design: Curt Diepenhorst
Cover photo: Ibushuev / Getty Images®
Interior illustration: © Jan Treger / 123RF®
Interior design: Katherine Lloyd/The DESK

First Printing August 2014 / Printed in the United States of America

To my husband Geoff. You are my best friend, inspirer, and forever love of my life. Thank you for pushing me to be brave. To my incredible children, Mike and Brittainy. You bring joy to my life every day. I'm so incredibly proud of you both. To my beautiful daughter-in-law Hilary, who brought us Maggie Claire and Mollie Rose. You are all three pure joy! To Harold and Doris, my wonderful mom and dad. Thanks for showing me what courage looks like.

To the incredible MOPS family and wonderful moms who shared your stories here, without whom this book couldn't have been written. You inspire me.

CONTENTS

Introduction

THE COMMON DENOMINATOR

I t was like a train wreck in slow motion. I felt myself pitch forward but couldn't do a thing to stop it. I threw my hands out in an effort to counter the freefall, but before I knew it I was sprawled on my hands and knees on the concrete sidewalk. Believe me, it wasn't a graceful fall, but a herky-jerky lunge that made Mandy and Carolyn, two friends walking beside me, gasp, "Are you okay?"

Okay? I wanted to pull the sidewalk up over my head and hide. I had slammed forward on my knees, with my rear end sticking up. To add insult to injury, I had dropped my purse and all manner of nonsense had rolled out. Sunglasses, cell phone, three ballpoint pens, and endless odds and ends of receipts and paper scraps all spilled out, announcing loudly, *Not only can this poor lady not walk, but she keeps a terribly messy purse.*

I looked accusingly at the sidewalk where I had been walking, no holes, no bumps, just smooth concrete. I had simply tripped over my own two clumsy feet, in heels that were too high. And now I had a broken toenail, a scuff on my pants, and a bruise on my ego. Carolyn and Mandy helped me pick myself up. I jammed the chaos back into my purse and we continued to the car.

We had just finished dinner at a beautiful lakeside restaurant in Grand Rapids, Michigan, and one of my companions, Carolyn, was a brand new friend. In fact we had just met that day, and the evening had been full of laughter and great conversation.

As we continued to walk to the car, Carolyn shared a story. As a publisher and editor, she often meets with authors and well-known leaders. Once, while standing and talking in a crowd of people, she took a step backward — big mistake. Before she knew it she was flat on her back, enveloped in an awkward silence as everyone around her averted their eyes and fidgeted, not quite sure what to do. What had caused her to fall? She wasn't quite sure, but what she did know was that her ankle hurt badly and she wanted out of there, fast.

Carolyn's story had no point other than to let me know she knew how I felt. As she shared the story and how embarrassing it was, we all laughed together and I felt our hearts bond over a common line of human frailty. She was saying, *Me too. I know what it feels like to fall in front of people you barely know.*

Later that evening Mandy shared a similar story. She had gone to the gym with a friend and was trying out a new piece of workout equipment. Showing off a little, she got moving a little too fast, slipped off, and took all the skin off both of her shins. Not only was it painful, but it took a long time to heal. A bit of the skin had been taken off of her pride as well.

Mandy's and Carolyn's stories made me thankful. They both knew I was embarrassed about falling, especially when there was no good reason for it. I was just being careless. Without a hint of ridicule or smugness they were both saying through their stories, *It happens to all of us. You're not alone.*

What an incredible feeling to know you are in good company, to know that other people share your experience and know how you feel. This is the first thing we hope to accomplish with this book. It's not a fat finger pointing in your face to say you shouldn't have fear. Nor is it a flippant "how not to worry" manual. Instead, it's a resounding statement: *We know what fear is like; we deal with it too.*

We all have fears and worries, some less, some more. The research backs this up. According to the National Institute of Mental Health, about forty million American adults age eighteen and older deal with an anxiety disorder in a given year, causing them to be filled with fearfulness and uncertainty.[1] And even though we know in our heads that many of our fears are silly, we still go there. Ninety percent of our fears are wasted on things that we ourselves deem "insignificant," and sixty percent are focused on things we know could never really happen.[2] But common sense doesn't often prevail. We worry anyway.

MOPS International (Mothers of Preschoolers) asked hundreds of moms some basic questions about their fears. MOPS has been helping moms through the stages of pregnancy, infancy, toddlerhood, and beyond to find friends through community and encouragement for over forty years. We *get* moms because we *are* moms. So we asked: What are your top three fears as a mom? When do you find yourself worrying the most and what do you do about it? How do you see fear affecting you most in your life? The response was overwhelming, ranging from *I occasionally worry about my child getting hurt* to *I worry constantly about every area of my child's life.* And the fear wasn't just focused on their children. Moms worry about themselves as a mom, not being good enough, not being enough for their children, and making mistakes that will scar their children for life. One mom's response was particularly poignant: *I can't seem to stop being afraid. I know my fears are ridiculous and unfounded, but I can't seem to get control of them. In fact, I feel like they control me.*

Why? Why do we do this to ourselves? Many of us feel we don't have a choice. Our thoughts suck us in. We see terrible things happening in the news every day: people losing their jobs and finding themselves homeless, children getting snatched by strangers or seriously injured playing sports, fires that consume homes or tornados that shred them to pieces. Even in our own circles we hear bad news: of the friend of a friend who lost her husband and now she has to figure out how to take care of five kids by herself, or the church acquaintance whose child has been diagnosed with a serious disability.

As moms, there are also other, more secret, fears that keep us up at night. Am I a good enough mom? What if my child doesn't like me? What if others don't like my child? What if I do something crazy that messes up my child forever? What if I'm not cut out to be a mom? What if I've *ruined my life forever*?

If you've ever dreamed up a crazy fear and then wondered where in the world it came from, you're not alone. It doesn't mean you are crazy, even though it can make you feel like you are. We all deal with fear, even the brave mamas with poker faces who never flinch. The things we fear may differ but inside we're all the same. Fear is real and it spares none of us.

And that's the point of this book. What I'd like you to do is pour yourself a steaming cup of coffee, curl your legs up on the couch, and get ready to ponder solutions as you travel the road of real life with us. I'll share stories of real moms, with real fears, who refuse to let fear run their lives. They don't pretend. They don't hide. Nor do they throw up their hands in defeat. And as you read, I hope you'll say, *Me too, I've been there.*

But not only do I want the stories to resonate, I want them to inspire you to ask, *So what will I do about it?* One day as I was talking to a friend about fear and worry, she shared this wisdom that I've considered many times: "Fear may come knocking at your door, but that doesn't mean you have to invite it in for dinner!" How true. How many times have I gotten caught up in a simple fear and let it ruminate in my head only to realize it had taken up residence in my heart? Yet I'm the one who guards the door to my head and my heart, just as you do yours. I have a choice and so do you. This book is meant to help you realize, appreciate, and implement your options when fear comes knocking so that you will not only not invite it in, but also barricade the door against it.

Here's why I think this book is so important. While being a mom is an incredible source of joy and fulfillment, it's also an opportunity for fear and worry to turn you into someone you don't even recognize. These beautiful little people that bless our homes can cause us to have irrational thoughts and go places in our minds that we didn't know were even there. So we're calling an end to the silent worries and secret fearful thoughts. No more sitting alone and feeling like we are the only ones who get carried away on the worry train without so much as a map or a toothbrush. We're going to face it openly and honestly. And with an honest look, healthy perspective and an arsenal of weapons will come.

We'll start by acknowledging the fears we know all moms deal with, sharing some of our research from MOPS International. We'll engage your heart with lots of mom stories, some funny and some raw, including everyone from the first-time mom just figuring out how to survive without sleep to the mamas who have traveled around the mommy block and ventured into grandma bliss (like me). Then we'll give you a gentle nudge with ideas on how you can grow. And we'll be there every step of the way.

If you've picked up this book, we'll consider you ready to get started, so let's begin right now. Close your eyes (after you read this paragraph) and picture it. Picture you, moving through an ordinary day and encountering scary circumstances or thoughts that stop you cold. See yourself, not being overwhelmed with fear or worry about the day ahead, but smiling with confidence as you consider all the good in store. See the new you, moving forward with confidence and not wasting time with worries that make your stomach hurt. And it's you, laying your head on the pillow at night, slipping easily into a deep and peaceful sleep.

Are you ready to take the next step toward the new courageous you? We thought so. Turn the page.

1

THE TRUTH
ABOUT FEAR

This fear thing is not just a new habit I picked up last night. I remember being newly married and more than once sitting up in bed in our first apartment in Houston, whispering frantically, "Honey, what was that noise? Get up and go see what it is! I think someone is breaking into the house!" Geoff, my poor husband, would sigh, dutifully get up, and trudge around our apartment in his pajamas checking every lock on every door. We have never owned a gun and so he sometimes jokingly said his only defense was to hope the intruders would take one look at his bed hair and mismatched pajamas and run screaming from the house.

It was easy to laugh at this in the light of day, but more difficult in the dark of night when noises were eerie and shadows were long. For a young bride far from home, locked doors were exceedingly important and I would obsess over them, sometimes checking them more than once if I was in our apartment alone. I remember one morning frantically searching for my keys, only to find I had left them in the lock on the outside of the door to our apartment *all night long*. Oh good grief, why hadn't I just put a sign on the door inviting all the neighborhood burglars in for a cup of coffee and a doughnut? I laughed about it at the time, but you can bet I made sure my keys were safely on the counter after that.

It got worse after my two children, Michael and Brittainy,

were born. What if someone broke in and stole the kids from their beds? Would we hear them? Would we wake up? Geoff would try to reason me out of my fear. "Sherry, have you ever known anyone that has had this happen? Have we ever had anyone even try to break in while we were sleeping?" The answer of course was no on both counts. I knew in my head Geoff was right. The chances of someone picking our house to break into were slim, especially when it was easy to see that we didn't have a lot of prize stuff to steal.

So why was I so fearful about someone breaking in? I was convinced if I wasn't careful about locking the doors or keeping the windows locked tight that something bad would happen. I felt compelled to ensure our safety, as if not checking the locks would somehow signal to all the bad people in the world to come running. Where did this compulsion come from?

As a little girl I remember my dad's nightly routine was to check every lock on every door as he went around turning off the lights for the night. (And might I note that turning off all the lights that I turn on is quite a job. My dad walks in my house today and says he's sure I'll be getting a Christmas card from the electric company as one of their prized customers.) My dad would go from door to door, his stocking feet softly padding on the carpet, and I would feel a sense of security as I heard the click of the deadbolt. *We're all safe and snug for the night.* I also remember a story my dad told of a trip to Chicago when all his stuff was stolen from the trunk of the car because he hadn't locked it. *Uh huh, when you are not careful, bad things happen.*

But this certainly wasn't my parents' fault. Locking your doors is just a wise precautionary move, and they were teaching me to be careful like good parents do. So when did I turn the corner from being careful to being fearful? I think it has something to do with my tightly clenched fists of control.

I noticed this tremendous need for control about fifteen years ago when I went on my first overseas mission trip. I was incredibly excited to get to visit a school for AIDS orphans in Kenya. But I had a problem. To get there required an eighteen-hour flight and I had a terrible fear of flying. I could handle short flights, although it required a peek into the cockpit to see if the pilot was indeed old enough to shave — and did I smell alcohol on his breath?

I wasn't a fan of bumpy air and felt completely out of control when the plane would bounce around. How long will this last? How bad was it going to get? I didn't have the answers and couldn't do anything but sit there and nibble on my miniature bag of five peanuts. Really, I was less focused on my fear of falling out of the sky and being smashed to bits than on my extreme need to end the turbulence. I knew in my head that turbulence was hardly ever the cause of injury or death. My dad had been an engineer for an aircraft company for forty years and had explained the science of flying to me many times. He also explained that bumpy air was nothing more than air pockets that the plane simply cut through. But for me, turbulence was scary, and I wanted to stop it *that very minute*. But I couldn't stop it. I wasn't in control.

I remember thinking if I had to sit strapped in that seat of torture all the way to Kenya, I would lose my mind. I pictured myself in seat 4B with clammy hands, heart jumping into my throat whenever an announcement came over the intercom, unable to relax my grip on the armrest. For eighteen excruciating hours? No thank you.

WHAT IS THIS THING CALLED FEAR?

Picture this: you are in your house alone watching television and you hear the front door open and bang against the wall. You jump off the couch. Your heart is racing and you stand frozen for a moment. Then you start to run but you don't know which way to run or why you are running. After a few seconds, you realize the wind caught the door and there really is no danger. But your heart is pounding so hard you can actually hear it. Without you doing anything intentional, your breathing increased, your muscles tightened, and the blood vessels in your eyes started pumping more blood to your pupils so they would expand so you could see better. Your hands started to sweat and your tummy jumped up into your chest. You are not going crazy; this is your body initiating the fight-or-flight response that is critical to any animal's survival.

So what is this weird thing called fear? God made our brains incredibly complex, to respond even before we're able to process the response — a part of the brain that's often referred to as the lizard or reptilian brain. Fear starts with a stimulus that triggers chemicals in the brain that signal your heart, blood, and muscles to get ready for quick action. These are called autonomic responses and we don't consciously control them.

The fact that this response is automatic is a good thing. These physical responses are there to help you survive a dangerous situation by preparing you to either run or fight for your life. We see it play out in our lives every day. If you are sitting in the stands at a game and see a baseball coming at your head, you either reach up quickly to catch the ball, or if you are nonathletic like me, you gasp, duck, and expect your husband to catch it for you. If you are stepping out onto the street and a car suddenly appears, you quickly jump back. If you are walking down a dark lonely street at night, the prickles on the back of your neck signal you to get out of there quickly and get to a safer location. Fear can indeed keep us safe.

Fear can also make us sick. According to Dr. Lissa Rankin, "When you're scared, your lizard brain also turns on the sympathetic nervous system (the 'fight-or-flight' response), causing the adrenal glands to release epinephrine and norepinephrine, which increase pulse, blood pressure, and affects other physiological responses. The secretion of these hormones leads to a variety of metabolic changes all over the body."[3] These changes can include an increase in stomach acid and a decrease in helpful digestive enzymes, bringing on diarrhea or constipation. Cortisol, which suppresses your immune system, is also produced.

Dr. Rankin sums it up like this: "When your body is in the stress response [caused by constant fear and worry], *it can't repair itself.* Bodily functions break down every day, but they can only repair themselves when the body is in a state of physiological cal relaxation. When the stress response is repetitively triggered, organs get damaged and the body can't fix them. The cancer cells we naturally make, which usually get blasted away by the immune system, are allowed to proliferate. The effects of chronic wear-and-tear on the human body take their toll, and we wind up sick."[4]

So we know that fear can act as a deterrent from danger, but it can also wreak havoc on our bodies. Not only that, it can mess with your mind. Fear can make you lose perspective and abandon your sense of reason. The crushing power of worry can turn your head to mush. This is why as moms we need to pay attention to the place fear has in our lives. Fear can affect our health. It can affect our mood and our resilience. Worst of all, it can affect the way we mother, as Liz, mom of two, discovered.

I Can't Stop Worrying: Liz's Story

When I became a mom, I also became an expert worrier—almost as if worrying was an unavoidable side effect of motherhood. Before we left the hospital I struggled to get the hang of nursing and I was so worried we would continue to struggle once we got home. My first child was colicky and nursing never went well. I finally gave up around the three-month mark, feeling like I'd thrown all that time away on worry, anxiety, and guilt.

Childhood should be at least *some* fun and games, right? But there was a time when I worried I was not measuring up as a mommy because deep down, I did not want to play Candy Land, Chutes and Ladders, or Hungry Hungry Hippo with my children.

I remember when my husband brought home the game of Memory and presented it with a big smile on his face. What an opportunity! What a chance to help my daughter learn and grow! I had a three-year-old, a one-year-old, and a full-time job outside the home. My to-do list was long and my patience was in short supply, but I wanted to be a "good" mom, the kind who would play brain-building games with her children.

But sadly, I did not have the kind of children who would placidly listen to the rules and participate in accordance with those rules. And I wasn't prepared for how challenging it would be just to set up the Memory cards. "Leave that alone! Just give me a minute—Mommy needs to set these cards up for you." Learning the simple rules of the game was easy enough for my little smarty pants, and once she had the basics down she became an accomplished cheater in no time.

I played the game a few times before I packed it

up and put it away where it wouldn't be found by little hands, *and I worried.* I couldn't even manage to engage my child in preschool game play. How was I *ever* going to measure up as a mom? If I didn't take the time to play games with her, would my little girl develop necessary life skills like negotiation, turn-taking, playing fair, and knowing how to lose graciously? *What kind of a mother doesn't play games with her children?*

As a mom, I've worried about everything from proper nutrition to the whereabouts of my children, to bleeding wounds in need of stitches. All of these are valid concerns that deserve my attention, but many of my mom worries boil down to one question: *Am I a good enough mom?* The greater my worry, the greater my anxiety; the greater my fear—*the shorter my fuse.* The majority of my worries—real or imagined—center on my family. When I allow myself to be overtaken by worry, I have less patience and loving kindness for my husband and children—those I love best and most want to protect. I've seen the look on my husband's and children's faces when I become one mean mama, and it's not pretty. I fuss over unimportant details like socks on the floor or dishes on the counter, and everyone feels the effect of my anxiety.

My most powerful defense against worry is prayer.

My worry, my deepest-darkest fear, is that I'm not a good enough mother to my children. The truth is I will never measure up to the ideal I believe my children deserve, but God is the perfect parent they need. When I give my weakness and worry over to him, I can rest assured knowing he's got my back—and my family's—and I don't have to be "good enough." I also rely on a few trusted mom friends for valuable feedback when I find myself asking, "What kind of a mom am I?" Sometimes I need validation (*I've done the same thing!*), sometimes I need advice, and sometimes I just need someone to listen without judgment.

One of my most trusted resources for hashing through worries is my husband. When I find myself absorbed by worry, I try to remember that I am not in this thing alone. Marriage and parenthood are something we do better together. ✻

WHO INVITED THE UGLY STEPSISTERS?

Worry and anxiety are closely related to fear, and I think of them as the ugly stepsisters. As in the case of Cinderella, the stepsisters were mean and nasty and up to no good. They constantly got in the way, stubbornly inserting themselves as roadblocks to Cinderella's peace of mind and happiness. This can be true of worry and anxiety as well, which are the related manifestations of fear. They can show up as nervous thoughts and overblown emotions, and disguise themselves as stomachaches and difficulty in making decisions. They can be the very antithesis of reasonableness.

Back to that mission trip to Kenya: I really wanted to make this trip. As I saw the pictures of the children's faces at the school, I knew God was pulling on my heart. I so wanted to help. My teacher's heart thrilled at the thought of preparing lessons that stirred their curiosity and inspired them to learn. I wanted to encourage the teachers and see for myself ways that we could be an ongoing source of help. But my thoughts went back and forth, up and down, like a crazy seesaw of emotions out of control. How could I possibly think about going? Kenya is so far away. How could I be away from my kids for two weeks with no way to quickly get back to them? But how could I not go? The faces of the children called my name. I desperately wanted to be a part of something bigger than me, to use my skills and resources to make a difference.

I began to think about all the things that could go wrong. My plane could crash. I could get sick from drinking the water and end up with a parasite that could eat through my intestines. (I have no idea where this worry came from since I had never heard of a parasite eating anyone's intestines.) Our van that would carry us from the airport to the school could break down and we might never make it to the school at all. What if I got malaria? What kind of animals were there and what if I got attacked by one? Whew, I really deserved an Academy Award for all the mama drama that was taking place in my brain.

As I allowed my mind to roam the road of possible disaster, I felt anxiety grip my stomach and worry take over my heart. Of course I couldn't go. There were just too many risks. I was perfectly happy where I was.

But I will never forget the day my fingers were poised on my computer keyboard as I prepared to send an email letting our mission's director know I couldn't go. At that moment, someone walked into my office and laid a check on the keys where my fingers had been. A wonderful friend who knew I was considering the trip had just paid my entire trip cost and had attached a note to the check that read, *I can't wait to see what God is going to do.*

I go back to that moment often when the fingers of fear try to take a grip on my heart. If I had followed where worry and anxiety were trying to take me and allowed fear to make my decision for me, I would have closed the door on an experience that changed me forever. I returned from the trip feeling like I was ruined for the ordinary, as if my very eyeballs had been exchanged for new ones that now saw the world differently. I returned with a heart broken for children who have lost their parents and deal with pain every day. I came back with a totally different perspective on what it means to have enough, and a driving desire to really care for those who don't. I came back with my puny heart stretched to near bursting, and I am so thankful.

But this is the power of fear and why I think it is one of the most destructive tools of Satan. He wants to blind us from what God wants to do in our lives. Satan can't thwart God's plans, but he can sure try to confuse and distract us away from what God is saying to us and what is true. Jeremiah 29:11 reminds us, "'For I know the plans I have for you,' declares the LORD, 'plans to prosper you and not to harm you, plans to give you hope and a future.'" This verse not only tells me that God is thinking about me, but he has a plan for me and it's a good one. God's not plotting disaster for me. He's on my side. Satan does everything he can to get me to forget this. That's why he throws the door wide open to the ugly stepsisters of worry and anxiety as often as he can.

What Does God Say?

I think it's time for us to be honest. We're all going to deal with fear, no matter how many hours we've spent in Sunday school or how long we've attended church. God is not surprised by our fear; in fact, God directly addresses fear in the Bible over three hundred times! In Psalm 56, David cries out, "When I am afraid, I put my trust in you." God doesn't try to hide the fact that we will have fear, and he never condemns or shames us because of it. While he does urge us to not let it take control of our lives or define who we are, he always gives us the why behind it.

> For I am the LORD your God who takes hold of your
> right hand and says to you, Do not fear; I will help you.
> (Isaiah 41:13)

> So do not fear, for I am with you; do not be dismayed,
> for I am your God. I will strengthen you and help
> you; I will uphold you with my righteous right hand.
> (Isaiah 41:10)

Even though I walk through the darkest valley, I will
fear no evil, for you are with me; your rod and your
staff, they comfort me. (Psalm 23:4)

Over a hundred verses in the Bible specifically tell us not to
fear, and they are written with the knowledge that life is full of
scary stuff that will cause the natural reaction of fear to rise up in
us. The point of the "fear not" is not a "shame on you" from God,
but rather, *Daughter, I know you are afraid; let me help.*

LET'S GET PRACTICAL

In the coming chapters, I invite you to join me in traveling the
road to recovery over fear. But the journey starts with acknowledging where you are today. Give yourself some space to consider the following questions. When you feel comfortable, sit
down with a friend and discuss your answers.

1. What are the things that you worry about the most?
   Try to put names to them (for example, turbulence,
   someone breaking in, fear that my child will be hurt).
   Where do these fears come from? Do they come from
   an experience or somewhere else?
2. How do I see fear showing up in my life? Is it affecting
   my habits (sleeping, eating, relaxing)? Is it affecting my
   relationships or decisions?
3. What do I feel like God might be trying to say to me
   through this chapter?

Let's Take Action

Start a "Facing Your Real Mom Fears Journal" and write down any thoughts you had as you read this chapter. Were there any moments that made you think *me too* as you read? Jot them down.

IN SEARCH
OF PERFECT

t was just me and him, this first child of mine. He lay sleeping soundly in my arms and I sat in the dark quiet of the hospital room listening to the rhythmic sounds of baby breaths, caressing the little cheek that felt like velvet. He was perfect. He was mine. And now it was time to bring him home.

The thought flicked through my brain, *I wonder if they know I don't know what I'm doing?*

They being the nurses who zipped in and out of my room with confident efficiency, checking Mike's breathing, taking detailed notes on his fluid intake and output. How long had he nursed and was I confident he had actually swallowed something? How many wet diapers had he had? I answered the questions in a bit of a daze, wondering if I was accurate with my answers. Had I changed two diapers or three? How was I supposed to know if I was breastfeeding correctly? I watched amazed as they swaddled him securely in his little blankets, like a little baby burrito with a sweet face. I laid him gently on my bed and tried to copy their movements. We ended up with a baby wad, the blankets knotted up and Mike's little arms flailing. The list of things I didn't know I should know was piling up fast.

Geoff, along with my mom and dad who were in town to celebrate their first grandbaby, walked into the hospital room. I watched proudly as my mom rocked and held Mike and declared him beautiful. I felt my heart swell with pride. He *was* beautiful. And he was mine.

But then I heard a sound that we would hear again and again over the next few weeks. The sound was part gasp, part gulp, and was coming from my tiny son. Startled, I sat up in the bed and looked at my mom, who cradled Mike in her arms. The noise sounded like a tiny bird frantically gasping for his last breath. What did it mean? Was he choking on something? The noise startled my mom as well and she quickly handed tiny Mike to his daddy. Geoff's eyes met mine and we shared a silent thought. *What in the world are we supposed to do?*

We rang for the nurse, who reassured us Mike was fine. As a newborn, his lungs were still immature, and while lying down, he might swallow and take in a breath at the same time, causing him to have a gasping reaction. *Perfectly normal* were the words the nurse used. She deftly reached for Mike as he made the noise again and turned him easily over in the palm of her hand, elevating his head to make it easier for him to breathe. As he began to relax she gently flipped him over in her hand with masterful ease, supporting his tiny head between her index and ring finger, and handed him back to me. She smiled at me as she said, "He's fine. You'll get used to all the little noises."

I had my doubts. We packed up the myriad of newly acquired items: the syringe to suction out Mike's nose, the formula samples, the teeny-tiny nail clippers so he wouldn't scratch himself, the little blue baby hat and mittens to keep his body heat in. Was there a list of how and when to use these things?

I swallowed down the first rumblings of panic in my throat as I was loaded in the wheelchair. *Oh, my Lord, they are actually going to let me take this baby home!* Holding my tiny, perfect son in my arms, I pasted a smile on my face, but I could feel my lips trembling. *Surely they will stop me before I make it out the door. They'll figure out I'm a know-nothing mommy who thought the nasal syringe was something you squeeze to cool the baby off with blasts of air, like a fireplace damper. Any minute now they will discover I'm a mommy imposter who pretends not to gag when changing a poopy diaper, and who wants to run the other way screaming when she sees spit-up.* I looked around as we came out of the elevator, expecting the baby police to stop me cold. *Ma'am, hand over the baby. You don't know what you're doing!*

But there were no baby police. No one stopped us. In fact, as I was whisked out the door, people smiled that sweet, *oh, a new mommy* smile. Inside I wanted to scream, to latch on to the sleeve of the nurse pushing my chair. *Don't let me go. I'm a mommy idiot! I can't be trusted!*

My first wave of fear hit. What if we were struck by a crazy driver on the way home and Mike's car seat wasn't strong enough? He looked so tiny, swallowed up by the head cushion and straps. Had I adjusted the straps to the right height? How in the world was I supposed to know?

We made it home and somehow made it through our first night. Mike in the tiny cradle beside our bed and me, lying three feet away just on the edges of sleep, ready to jump up with the first cry. I remember thinking the next morning what a beautiful thing sleep was, emphasis on *was*.

As I stood in front of the kitchen sink the next morning, I

looked at the display of bottle nipples, screw-on lids, and plastic liners laid out on a clean towel next to the sink. In accordance to the thinking of that time, I was to make sure Mike drank some water in addition to nursing him every two to three hours. How much? I hadn't written it down. And it *was* water, wasn't it? I was pretty sure the pediatrician hadn't said coffee. No, that was for me.

I was positive the other parents in our prenatal class had paid better attention than we had. They all had seemed so confident, asking questions about the merits of breastfeeding and discussing the latest brands of baby monitors. I remembered the instructor talking about how our baby's cry would mean different things and how before too long we would be able to sense the tone and urgency, and be able to decipher exactly what our baby was saying.

But what if I couldn't? What if, in my exhaustion, I slept right through his cries? And if I did hear him, what if I tried everything and couldn't get him to stop? The thoughts of *what if, what then* swam through my weary brain. I so wanted to be that perfect mom, who pushed out a baby in an hour and wore her size-six jeans home from the hospital; who whipped up homemade baby food in the blender for her baby who always slept through the night; who kept a clean, germ-free house and always had enough diapers in her perfectly organized diaper bag to share with all the other mommies. But as life would have it, I turned out to be the mommy who had to wear her sister-in-law's stretchy gym pants home from the hospital, who couldn't even find her blender in her messy kitchen, who would give an occasional swipe to the counters with an antiseptic wipe and call it good, and who once found her own shoe—which had been missing for a week—in the diaper bag.

Thank goodness there are other moms like me. Mandy, mom of three, shares her story of her dream of perfection long gone.

I Used to Dream of Perfect: Mandy's Story

It had been the hottest summer on record in Northern California, and we were new to town. I hadn't had an opportunity to meet many new friends, and since we didn't have anywhere special to be that summer, I decided that it was the perfect time to attempt potty training my two-and-a-half-year-old son, Joseph. I figured that if we just focused for a couple of days we might be able to master it. So I employed the technique taught by a European friend, who told me that the fastest way to potty train was to have your kiddo live naked for a few days. And because I am a sucker for expedited potty training and also for cute baby buns, we tried it. It was 95 degrees every day that summer, so forgoing clothing wasn't a huge sacrifice for him. After a few days, Joseph had gotten the hang of the potty routine, and I felt accomplished, like I had mastered this motherhood thing.

A few days later, a mom down the street invited Joseph and me to join her and some friends at a park nearby. I was excited to make some mom friends and Joseph was excited because the park had a lazy river that toddlers could sit and splash in. Water is always a good idea and sure to entertain kids for at least fifteen minutes so that moms can breathe and maybe grab a quick sip of coffee.

But as soon as I showed up I started to judge myself. The other moms drove nicer cars and had certainly taken a shower that morning. They seemed to have it all together. I, on the other hand, had forgotten sunscreen, and the snacks I brought weren't in perfectly proportioned bento boxes or cut into star shapes. The other moms had beautiful, plush beach towels; I grabbed five-year-old bath towels off the floor. I could just feel all the perfect moms looking down their noses at me. Thinking about how much better suited they were to raise a human being. I mean, I couldn't even remember sunscreen!

Things went okay for a while; the moms chatted while the kids played. I continued to play mind games with myself about how perfect the other moms were. And then it happened. I looked over to the lazy river, and there was Joseph, completely naked, and peeing a consistent stream over another child's head straight into the lazy river.

Apparently we missed a few of the nuances of potty training.

While all of the other moms ran to remove their children from the now-contaminated water, Joseph and I calmly packed up our things and headed home for nap time. We left the park that day pink in the cheeks, Joseph from the lack of sunscreen, and me from embarrassment. For days after, my ego was bruised and my inner dialogue was stuck on repeat, convincing me that I would never be a perfect mom. I felt like I would never measure up to the standards that other moms somehow achieved effortlessly. Would I ever be able to teach my kids everyday skills like peeing in a potty? I implemented the only technique I knew and prayed desperate prayers that my imperfect parenting wouldn't ruin my kids forever. ✸

THE THINGS THAT HAUNT US

It's perfectly natural to feel fear when facing new experiences. The first time we live on our own is a daunting experience. We have to learn to shop on a budget, cook for ourselves, and get along with roommates. We face new things over and over throughout our lives, each one presenting new challenges and problems to solve. But creating a new life in your body and then introducing him into your life and family is an experience like no other. Besides getting adjusted to your new role as a mom, you may also face a different financial situation, physical changes to your body, relationship changes with your husband

and family, professional changes, disruptions to daily routine, and sleep deprivation. Just as the first weeks of living on your own posed new challenges, bringing a child into your family can raise some natural but stressful fears. Let's take a moment to look at a few new mom fears.

Am I Up for This?

This is a natural question that I think all new moms face. You wonder if you have what it takes. If, when you are running on your last ounce of steam, you'll fold like a cheap accordion. The questions can also run deeper like mine did, when I would ask myself, *But what if I'm not cut out to be a mom? What if, in my lack of knowledge and experience, I mess up my child?* Living with a baby isn't the same as getting accustomed to a new roommate. This is big stakes, with the well-being of my child on the line. What if I can't learn all the things I need to know? What if I stink at being a mom?

Here's the truth I've learned, even if it took awhile for the truth to really sink in. God came up with this concept of babies being born to their mommies, being born into a family. And he designed this with intentional care. In fact, each of us is made carefully, with much thought and purpose:

> For you created my inmost being; you knit me together in my mother's womb. I praise you because I am fearfully and wonderfully made; your works are wonderful, I know that full well. My frame was not hidden from you when I was made in the secret place, when I was woven together in the depths of the earth. Your eyes saw my

unformed body; all the days ordained for me were written in your book before one of them came to be. (Psalm 139:13 – 16)

Not only did God think about me when he made me, but he thought about my entire life and my future, which included the parents that I would have. This verse not only applies to you but to *your baby* as well. God knew you would have the children you have. He created them. He gave them to you. Here's the great news: this also means he fully equips you to be their mom. He doesn't just toss you children and then throw up his hands as if to say, *Well, I wonder how that will turn out.* He gave you the exact right temperament, the intelligence, the skills, and the patience to be the exact right mom for your children. While you won't be *a perfect mom*, you already are *the perfect mom for your kids.*

Will I Make the Same Mistakes My Parents Did?

You probably will. But because of the mistakes your parents made, you will also be intentional about doing better in the areas that really matter to you. If you wish your mom had told you more often that she thought you were pretty or smart, you will very likely intentionally do this with your children. If you wish your dad would have hugged you more or spent more time with you, the chances are you will make sure this happens in your own family. It's a ridiculous lie of Satan that we have to be what our parents are, or anybody else for that matter. God designed you to be you. Some of us had incredibly hard parts of our childhood, but the good news is that we can give our own children what we found lacking when we were growing up.

What If I Can't Stop Being Selfish?

The reality is we can't stop being human. And since we live with ourselves every day, we also think about ourselves every day. Being a mom doesn't mean you stop being you. It means you adjust to make your life bigger, to open your heart wider, to love even deeper. But being a mom in no way means you forget about your own needs. In fact, our research at MOPS International shows that the best moms are the ones who pay attention to their own needs, which include having and making time for friends; paying attention to their marriage; taking care of their emotional, physical, and social needs; and providing for their spiritual development. In many ways, your baby will disrupt your day, your schedule, and your sleep. But you are still you, and your physical, emotional, social, and spiritual needs are still important. Paying attention to these is not selfish; it's wisdom.

What If My Child Turns Out Like Me?

This is a loaded question, isn't it? We are so proud when our daughter develops our beautiful blue eyes or flashes her daddy's feisty smile. But what about those things we desperately wish weren't a part of us? What if by nature or nurture, we unwittingly pass these things along to our kids?

I remember Geoff telling me a story of getting so angry as a young child that he kicked out the glass door at his church. This story struck fear in my heart, because I had anger issues too. I remember getting so angry at my older brother that I hid straight pins in the carpet of the doorway to his room so he would step on them with his bare feet. I even hesitate to share this story, lest you, dear reader, declare me a horrible person! Imagine my fear when I thought about passing this horrible, out-of-control anger on to my son and realizing that he was getting a double dose from both my husband and me.

But here's the truth: just as you have parts of your personality that have brought you challenges, so will your children. You have learned to address them and grow through them, and you may still be working through them. So will your child. Your struggles and challenges will make you more sensitive to this. When we noticed that Mike would become so angry that he couldn't express himself any other way than throwing himself on the ground, we coached him to slow down and take a breath. We gave him space to calm down. We helped him put words to his feelings and let him know we understood what it feels like to be out of control. We were able to help him manage his anger because we had learned to do these things ourselves.

The Three Beautiful Truths
of Mommyhood

I think back often to that day I brought Mike home from the hospital, with a new mommy heart full of fear. I worried I would never be a good enough mom. I worried I would surely ruin this perfect child. There were moments when I knew I was doing things that he would later be telling his therapist or Oprah (for the whole world to hear). Mike is now a man of twenty-seven, with two beautiful daughters of his own. He is still upright and breathing, of sound mind and body. Despite my fears, I didn't ruin him or his sister who joined our family four years later. I have though, through the joyful moments and the hard lessons, learned what I call the Beautiful Truths of Mommyhood.

1. There is no "perfect" to achieve.

I love this beautiful truth because it is full of mercy. I so wish I had embraced this truth earlier in my momhood and gotten the picture of a perfect mom out of my head. I wasted a lot of time yearning to be the mom next door who, from my vantage point, looked perfect. I wasted days beating myself up, only to realize that to be the best mom I could be was the best for my kids. They needed me, imperfect, uncertain me. And what was really interesting to discover was that the so-called perfect mom next door wasn't so perfect. She had doubts and struggles and times when she felt like she had no answers at all either. Just because I couldn't see them didn't mean they weren't there.

I've learned to trust that God truly does know what he is doing. He gave me my kids, and made me who I am. He knows cleaning countertops isn't my favorite job and he knows I let the laundry pile up. Now, at the end of a bad day that makes me feel like I'm not the best, I run to the One who loves me best.

2. Great moms don't happen by accident.

This truly is a beautiful truth because it's filled with hope. Great moms don't happen by accident, like a lottery that I'm destined to lose, but they do happen with intention. And there are many intentional things I can do to be my best. I can surround myself with other moms who understand my imperfectness and challenge me to be my best and encourage me when I'm not. There are great books on parenting that I can read and great mom organizations to be a part of, like MOPS International. Being a mom is challenging, but there's no reason to do it alone. Look within your social circles or church to find an older mom who can be a trusted friend to talk to, who can put her arm around you and assure you that you will surely make it through the challenging days.

3. God's got my back.

You may have had experience with a church that gave you the picture of a harsh, unforgiving God who is impossible to please. Or you may have grown up without any knowledge of God at all. Here's the truth that is a game changer for every mom. The God who made you is crazy in love with you. Listen to these beautiful words designed to soothe any weary mom's heart.

> The LORD your God is with you, the Mighty Warrior who saves you. He will take great delight in you; in his love he will no longer rebuke you, but will rejoice over you with singing. (Zephaniah 3:17)

I don't know about you, but people don't fall on the ground in a swoon when I walk into a room. Rarely do I feel like my family is so delighted in me that they rejoice over me. In fact, there have been days when I've wondered if they even like me! But my God does. He made me and called it good. He wants me to succeed as a mom. He thinks about me every day and is delighted, even when I blow it as a mom, even when my heart is filled with fear.

LET'S GET PRACTICAL

1. What were your thoughts and feelings when you brought your first baby home from the hospital? Did you feel confident or were you full of uncertainty?
2. Did any of the fears mentioned in the chapter resonate in your heart? Were there any others that were not mentioned that you struggle with?
3. Do you have a hard time believing any of the Beautiful Truths? Which one, and why do you think this is?
4. What do you feel God might be saying to you through this chapter?

LET'S TAKE ACTION

If you don't have one already, consider finding a mom mentor. You can use a mom mentor in more than one way: to encourage you, to be your prayer partner, to talk about her experience in an upcoming stage of life you will be facing with your children, or to help you grow in specific parenting or life skills.

3

ARE MY FEARS
REASONABLE?

The parenting website Babycenter.com recently polled 2,400 parents to ask them about the things they feared most regarding their children. It led them to ask the question: "Are our kids really at risk, or is worry simply woven into our parental DNA?"[5] Great question. I've often wondered if my fears about my kids are based on any rational reality at all, or if I deserve a trophy with my name on it that declares me the world's most creative worrier.

I remember feeling very anxious when my son Michael had his first really high fever. He started out as just cranky, but then I noticed he became more listless. His temperature registered at slightly over a hundred, but over the next hour started to spike up to 102. I called his pediatrician, who agreed that a quick assessment of the situation might be needed, so he made room for Mike on his schedule. As we bundled tiny Mike into the car, fear gripped my heart. What if this was something really serious, like meningitis? My mind scrambled to think of the things I had read about this malady. What were the other symptoms? Had I noticed anything else that I had failed to mention to the doctor?

When we arrived at the pediatrician's office, we were met with calm efficiency. "Please sign in and have a seat. We'll let the doctor know you are here."

My body did indeed sit down, but inside my emotions were standing up and screaming, *Can't you see my baby needs help?*

Only a few minutes passed in the waiting room, but to me it seemed like an hour as my mind explored all the possibilities. *How high of a fever is too high? Should I have brought him in sooner? What is the doctor going to say and am I prepared to hear it? I wish the doctor would hurry up! We have to get Mike in there this instant! No, I don't want to go in. I'm afraid of what he might say.* I imagined all manner of diagnosis, from really serious to life threatening.

Finally we were called in. The doctor examined Mike, looking in his ears and examining his throat, then calmly said, "Mike has an ear infection. Let's start him on an antibiotic."

What? The questions tumbled forth. How did he get this? What should I have done to prevent it? How much pain was he in and should I have noticed it sooner?

I'll never forget the way our kind pediatrician pulled his rolling doctor stool over to where I was sitting with Mike cradled in my arms. He looked me right in the eye and calmly reassured me everything was okay. Mike probably did have some discomfort in his ears, but he was sleeping soundly, which indicated the pain wasn't severe. He would prescribe the antibiotic and the nurse would talk to me about how much infant pain reliever to give him. He reassured me that a temperature was an indicator of some sort of infection or virus and needed to be addressed, but it wasn't an automatic reason to panic. He then talked to me about the way germs and viruses worked and why we wouldn't want to shield our children from all of them. They built up resistance in the body and strengthened the immune system, sort of like a military general rallying the troops. He talked about how fevers usually run their course and while it's always good to consult your pediatrician, not every fever needs an antibiotic.

I so appreciated the pediatrician's wise words. He knew my new mommy instinct was to try to prevent illness and control everything about Mike's environment. He also knew this wasn't a good thing. He reassured me that Mike would come in contact with germs. He would have more fevers in his lifetime. This was the way his body was designed. And it was good.

But back to the question posed by Babycenter.com, do fear and worry always go hand in hand with parenting? And are we worrying about reasonable things? The article pointed out that parents and nonparents alike tend to fear the things they can't control. Fear itself is often based on things that manifest themselves right in front of us, and we are prompted to react. In the case of Mike's fever, I could tell he wasn't feeling good. I read the temperature on the thermometer. It sent alarm bells off in my head. My doctor assured me that I did the right thing by calling him. But did my mind really need to go to the extremes, like already assuming Mike had a serious condition?

Parents today are barraged with extreme stories in the news, on television, and on the Web. When we hear of a story about an outbreak of measles at an elementary school halfway across the country, we immediately think about our own child's school. When we hear about a college student contracting meningitis from being exposed to close living conditions in the dorm, we think, *That could have been my child.* Alfred Sacchetti, an emergency room doctor in Camden, New Jersey, says, "Unfortunately, a lot of what we're exposed to on TV is designed to generate ratings rather than educate parents. Our access to information doesn't keep up with our access to entertainment."[6] I saw this with my own experience. I had heard of cases of high fever being a sign of meningitis, but I learned later that meningitis is rare. Not something to let your mind leap to as the first diagnosis.

According to Dictionary.com, fear is "a distressing emotion aroused by impending danger, evil, pain, etc., whether the threat is real or imagined." A step further is the definition of worry: "to torment oneself with or suffer from disturbing thoughts; to fret." In other words, we are faced with something scary (Mike's fever) and we feel fear. When I let my mind imagine the disastrous possibilities of what could happen (meningitis), I now allow my mind (and body) to be tormented by worry.

But I'm not alone in my worrying. As Dr. Alfred Sacchetti points out, we do tend to drift into the extreme worry category with our parent fears: "It's common for parents to worry more about their child being abducted by a stranger than about his riding in a car without a seat belt or playing near an ungated swimming pool — even though car and water-related accidents pose a far greater threat to kids than abduction."[7] In other words, parents are allowing themselves to be swept away by worrying about something that poses a minute risk. The article pointed out that to keep worry at bay, it's important to stick to the facts and focus on the proactive things you can do to minimize the dangers for your child.

So what do moms worry most about? We polled hundreds of moms through our MOPS Facebook page and blog and we asked some simple questions: What do you worry about as a mom and where do you think this fear came from? After categorizing the data (not all fears were expressed the same but many were similar), we came up with the Top Five Fears of Moms with Young Children, which somewhat matched the nationwide Top Parenting Fears on Babycenter.com. Let's take a minute and talk about each one of them.

What if I'm not enough?

Fear #1: I'm afraid I won't have enough money or resources to cover everything for the future

In our survey, I was surprised that this ranked as a top mom fear above health concerns or accidents, but I think it gets at the heart of a deeper root worry: Will I be a good enough mom to provide everything my child needs? This is fueled by pressure we put on ourselves, but also by our surrounding media. Our brain is bombarded with the messages that we must buy our children the newest educational toy and expose them to the latest early reading programs so they will reach their fullest potential. As moms, we feel pressure that we have to give everything to our children in order for them to achieve their best. Pamela Paul, journalist and author of *Parenting Inc.*, believes that this parental anxiety is fed by a scary economic climate and says, "Parents are afraid their children won't have an easy go of it because they aren't having an easy go of it. Many parents today are struggling to make ends meet, and they want a different kind of future for their kids."[8]

Every mom wants to be the best mom she can be and give the best advantages to her child. As moms we worry that our economic situation may limit our children and we sometimes translate this into "I'm not a good mom." But setting your child up for success doesn't always translate to money, and you shouldn't be panicking that your child is not on the list for an Ivy League school.

Tracey, a mom of two, shared this story: "We grew up poor, but I didn't know it. Looking back, I'm sure lack of income must have stressed out my mom, who raised us as a single parent. But as kids, my brother and sisters and I never felt like we didn't have enough. I'm sure more money would have made my mom's life easier, but we felt safe and loved. We didn't eat out, we didn't get expensive gifts for Christmas or birthdays, but my mom made life fun. We made up our own board games out of construction paper and pennies and we told stories and drew pictures to go with them. Now as a mom with kids of my own, I try to parent like my mom did. She didn't burden us with the lack of money but she was honest when we couldn't afford something. I want to give this same gift to my kids. Money isn't the same as love and more than anything I want my kids to know how much I love them."

Tracey's mom was a wise mama. Money isn't the same as love. But it's understandable that we worry about money when we read the news about scary economic times and the unemployment rate. A young mom of four shared this story: "My dad got laid off from his job in construction when I was seven years old. I remember how old I was because it was only two months before my eighth birthday. I remember getting nervous when my parents told me and I remember wondering if I would still get a birthday cake and the bike I had asked for. To this day I worry what will happen if me or my husband lose our jobs. Will we have enough to pay the bills? Will my kids have to go without? I know having a lot of money doesn't make me a good mom, but what if there's something my kids need and I can't afford to give it to them?"

This young mom phrased it beautifully. *I know having a lot of money doesn't make me a good mom, but what if ... ?* It's natural to let our mind go to worst case scenarios with losing the security of a job, and it's not just money we worry about. At the core of this fear we worry about being enough as a mom to provide everything our children will need. I recently talked with a mom who was getting ready to have her first baby and she said over the last six months she had begun to regret that she hadn't finished college. She shared, "I always wanted to be a teacher and work with children but I never finished my teaching degree. I work at a school now as a teaching assistant, but I'm limited in my job and how much money I can make. I've dreamed for years about having a baby. Now I worry that I'll be enough of a mom. Am I smart enough? Will I let my child down?" As she shared, I saw the longing in her face to have the ability to be more, provide more, to be the best mom that this baby would ever need or want. I hear this echoed over and over as I talk with moms. They have dreams for their child. They want to provide all the love and support and material things that their child will need to be all that God designed them to be. And the truth is they can and it depends very little on how much money they earn or how educated they are.

Our MOPS research with Barna backs this up. In partnership with Barna we surveyed three hundred MOPS moms and identified the top five attributes that make a better mom. We found that the time she invested in herself in the following areas made a critical difference:

1. Investing in her core emotional resilience and her own emotional health
2. Building a strong marriage, or if she is not married, investing in a relationship with a strong supporting partner
3. Investing in friendships with mentors and other moms
4. Developing her parenting finesse and practical mothering skills
5. Prioritizing her own spiritual development

Our research showed that when the mom invested in these five areas, it did more for impacting her mothering (and her children) than any other factors, including her economic situation or educational background. Why is this? It's because it's the strength of the mom herself that impacts the child, not her level of education or the amount in her checkbook. And the great news is that EVERY mom can invest in the things that will help her grow into the best mom her child would ever need or want, without going back to school or spending a dime. At MOPS we know that all of these attributes are greatly impacted by the last one on the list, her spiritual development. Her relationship with God gives her the resilience to face the pressures of being a mom and the confidence to face whatever will come her way. This is why MOPS groups are developed in partnership with the local church, a great place to take that next step toward Christ, in the safe environment of other moms who can give support and friendship while growing together as moms.

We need to remind ourselves as moms that time spent in fear or worry about how many material things we are able to give our child or whether or not we can afford the most expensive opportunities is wasted time. Investing in ourselves as healthy moms is much more productive.

STRANGER DANGER

Fear #2: I worry that my child will be snatched by a stranger

I will have to admit that I have spent far too much time worrying about this.

Many years ago, before he got married, my brother Ron lived with us, and he loved to spend time with my two kids. When the Ringling Brothers circus came to the Houston Astrodome, Ron offered to take both Mike and Brittainy. They were elated and couldn't wait for the evening to begin. As I helped four-year-old Brittainy get dressed, I talked with her about the importance of staying close to Uncle Ron and not wandering off by herself. She listened carefully and nodded her head in agreement.

Geoff and I had a dinner date with friends that evening and we met the kids back home at the end of the night. My brother, being the wonderful uncle that he was, had spoiled the kids with style. I heard about the red and blue slushies (and saw the evidence on Brittainy's front) and admired the light-up ringmaster's sword and stuffed elephant that Ron had splurged on. What I didn't hear about until the next day was what had happened while they were at the souvenir table.

While my brother was paying for the treats, Brittainy wandered away from the table to look at something. When she came back, Ron and Mike were gone. My brother, in the meantime, finished paying and looked around for Brittainy, but he couldn't find her. He frantically called her name and walked back and forth but didn't see her. Holding onto Mike, Ron started to *run* in the direction he thought Brittainy might have gone. Not finding her immediately, he did the wise thing and flagged down a security guard standing nearby. Minutes later they located another security guard who indeed had seen a little girl with blue slushy on her dress, standing alone in the sea of people, crying dejectedly. She was safe in the care of the security guards. Ron said the incident scared him so badly that he had nightmares afterward.

He wasn't the only one. When I heard this story, my blood iced up in my veins. My Brittainy. Alone. In a sea of who-knows-what-kind-of-people. For years after this, I wasted time worrying about the "what ifs" when my kids were out of my sight and warning them over and over to not talk to strangers or wander off by themselves. My mind went back again and again to *what could have happened*, and I allowed it to strike unreasonable fear in my heart. Taking wise precautions and being safe is good. Letting your mind ruminate on fearful scenarios and overanxious thoughts is not.

This fear of someone hurting or snatching your child is one of the most basic parental instincts, and it's not surprising that it ranked as number two in the survey of what moms fear. We hear horrible stories of kidnappings on the news and it strikes fear in our hearts. We start to wonder if we can even let our children out of the house to play in the yard.

I have a nephew who is a young adult now, but when he was four, he had a fixation on the concept of "strangers," resulting from a well-meaning discussion at his preschool. He would walk up to random people at church and ask point-blank, "Are you a stranger?" Many times the person was caught off guard, and not knowing Brandon, they would say, "Well, I guess so." Brandon would immediately run from the room screaming.

We want our children to be safe, but we don't want them to have unreasonable fear. Here's the reality. According to a 2013 *Washington Post* article, "children taken by strangers or slight acquaintances represent only one-hundredth of 1 percent of all missing children. The last comprehensive study estimated that the number was 115 in a year."[9] I think we can all agree that this is 115 too many, and we are moved to do anything we can to prevent this from happening to any child, whether they belong to us or not, but the chances of it happening to our child are very, very small. According to News. Discovery.com, a 2013 report shared, "Child abductions are a real threat, but the risk should be kept in perspective to avoid unnecessarily alarming parents and children."[10] In his book, *Protecting the Gift*, child-safety expert Gavin De Becker pointed out that compared to a stranger kidnapping, "your child is vastly more likely to have a heart attack, and child heart attacks are so rare that most parents (correctly) never even consider the risk."[11]

But yet we continue to worry. Remember that fear can be constructive when it acts like an alarm system, helping you identify dangerous situations before they arise so you lessen the risks. Your mom instinct will prompt you to talk to your children about being safe in situations where strangers will be present and talking your children through scenarios of being offered candy or a ride from someone that they do not know. We need to be careful, but we don't need to let our mom fear keep us from enjoying our children, nor should we cause undue fear in their hearts. It starts with gauging the amount of healthy fear we have versus the leap our thoughts may want to take into unnecessary worry about things that will likely never happen.

I recently had a conversation with a group of moms about this topic of our children wandering off and worrying about encounters with strangers. We each shared some panicky moments when we looked around and couldn't find our child in a store or public event. One mom shared about almost going over the brink of hysteria when she couldn't find her toddler at the grocery store, screaming to her other children "Where's Addie, where's Addie?" Her seven-year-old calmly said, "Mom, you are holding her." And indeed she was. Addie was calmly sitting on her hip, chewing on her sunglasses. She realized at that moment she needed to take a deep breath and slow down a bit. Sometimes life moves at such a frenzied pace and our reactions can be frenzied as well. She said that night before going to bed she took a few minutes to talk to God about her tendency to panic and asked for his peace even in the moments of crazy mom panic.

While "stranger danger" is real, we need to remind ourselves that God has his hand not only on our children, but on our mom hearts as well.

MY CHILD'S SAFETY

Fear #3: I'm afraid my child will be hurt in an accident

The bad news is accidents do happen. The good news is that you can do a lot to prevent these injuries. Dr. Alfred Sacchetti, chief of emergency services at Our Lady of Lourdes Hospital in Camden, New Jersey, says, "The vast number of accidental trauma accidents are preventable."[12] We have easy access to car seats, seat belts, and bike helmets. It's wise to talk to your child about using these items consistently and correctly and to model it yourself. It's wise to also make sure that when your child is with other people, these items will be consistently used.

But what if you utilize all the safety measures available and your mind still wants to go down the panic path? A few months ago, I woke up in the middle of the night worrying about Brittainy, now in college, because I knew she was going to be out late. Was she using her seat belt? What if she was hit by a car and couldn't call us? I woke Geoff up with a nudge and said, "Do you think Brittainy is okay? I don't like her having to walk to her car alone and driving this late at night." Geoff mumbled some sleepy yet profound words. "Perhaps you could take a vacation from worrying."

What an interesting concept. When we go on vacation, we do what needs to be done to get ready. We request time off work. We pack. We make arrangements for the dog and the newspaper. We take all the necessary precautions to ensure we will have a great vacation, from making the reservations to planning the schedule and itinerary. Then we go and enjoy ourselves. That's the point of a vacation. You get ready and then you trust that all the prep work you did will pay off.

I'm learning to do this with my worries about things I can't really control. There are preventative things I can invest in and invest in them I should, if it could make my child or family safer. But continuing to worry after I've done all I can doesn't keep anyone safer. In Brittainy's case, she always wears her seatbelt, and we've taught her to be a conscientious driver. Now it's time to trust and take a vacation from the frantic thoughts.

The other component of a vacation that I'm trying to apply is otherwise occupying my mind. When you go on a great vacation, you don't think about the day-to-day details of your house or work because there are so many other wonderful things to think about. What great restaurant should we try? What new adventure will we tackle tomorrow? These things are so much fun to think about, and on vacation we give ourselves permission to indulge in them to our heart's delight.

I'm learning that I can give my mind this same permission when faced with a worry. When Brittainy comes to mind, all wrapped up in a big worry, I can choose to think about the good. *Brittainy is a good driver. She's careful and thoughtful. She makes good choices.* The apostle Paul knew what he was talking about when he urged us to focus our minds on the positive: "Finally, brothers and sisters, whatever is true, whatever is noble, whatever is right, whatever is pure, whatever is lovely, whatever is admirable — if anything is excellent or praiseworthy — think about such things." (Philippians 4:8) I'm learning to keep this verse at the ready and give myself permission to indulge in the types of thoughts it suggests.

HOW CAN I PROTECT MY CHILD FROM OTHER KIDS?

Fear #4: I'm afraid my child won't fit in socially or will get picked on

This is a very real fear and hard to dismiss especially when we hear stories of how bullying has made other children miserable. As a mom it's painful to think about situations where my child won't be welcome or will face ridicule or meanness. It's unthinkable to me that people, young and old, would be purposefully cruel to each other. But it happens.

As a mom, I need to focus on what I can control and influence. I can control our home environment, teaching my child how to treat others based on the way we treat each other. I can keep an eye on the other environments that my child spends time in when I'm not with them. I can keep an open dialogue with my child to help them talk about what's going on so I can help them if a situation or relationship is not healthy. I can make sure my child knows that our home is a safe place and we love each other no matter what. Through conversations on tough questions I have the opportunity to teach my child crucial life skills that will help them the rest of their lives. *What do I do when someone doesn't like me? How can I make friends in new or difficult situations? What do I do when I bump up against someone who is really mean?*

What I can't control is what other people will think about my child and how they will react to my child in every situation. But I can influence how my child reacts back to them, and also what sinks into their heart.

As assistant principal of a large public elementary school, I unfortunately saw bullying occur on a regular basis. What was interesting to me was how it was aimed indiscriminately at all types of children. Chubby, skinny, quiet, popular, quirky — it seemed no one was completely spared. But who would the bully try to settle on? It was usually the child that didn't have the skills to confidently put the bully in his or her place. As a parent of two kids of my own, I made a few observations: (1) there will come a time when my child will get picked on, and (2) as a mom I can help them be ready.

I remember a conversation I had with a mom of a daughter who was entering fourth grade. The mother had observed her daughter having trouble finding someone to play with on the playground. She insisted that I move her daughter to another classroom, saying, "It's hurting my heart to see her so lonely." When I talked with the child, however, she didn't seem at all concerned. She was a happy, confident little girl, who seemed to like her class and teacher. I talked with the mom again and suggested we watch closely and give it a little more time. Within a month the little girl had made several friends and seemed relaxed and happy. When her mom asked her about it she replied, "I just told them I'd like to be their friend and asked if they'd like to be mine, like you told me to."

When it comes to fears and worries about our children not fitting in or being bullied, it's a natural mom instinct to power up and control the situation. Our "mama bear" rises up within us and we can quickly lose perspective or over-identify with our child's social circumstances. This is where our mom fear can carry us away. But here's a truth I've learned: difficult social situations can be the best moments of learning for my child. If I try to completely prevent or control them, I thwart the growth that comes from solving problems independently. Every child needs the opportunity to do this, with the comfortable guidance of a mom who refuses to get carried away with her fears.

HEALTH ISSUES

Fear #5: I'm afraid my child will have a serious illness or disability

This is a fear that can be paralyzing to our mom hearts. What if my child develops a serious health issue like diabetes or a heart condition? What if my child is born with a disability that I can't do anything about? As a mom, we want to stop anything that could hurt our child and we want to control every situation that causes them pain or difficulty. But the reality is, sometimes we can't.

I remember worrying about this before each of our children was born. What if they aren't healthy? Will I be able to handle it? If you are an expectant mom, let me share some statistics to put your mom heart at ease. According to parents.com, the statistics show that your baby has an overwhelming chance of being born perfectly healthy.[13] In the United States, only 4 percent of babies are born with any kind of health issue and this includes minor issues such as having an issue with a toenail or temporary problem with their heart that goes away soon after birth.

But it's normal as a mom to worry when you read stories of children born with serious health issues or disabilities and it's even more normal to wonder how you will handle it. And if your child does have a health issue, hearing that it's uncommon doesn't help settle your heart.

But for moms, God's plan is big. I recently talked with Megan, a mom of a beautiful daughter born with Down's syndrome. She said it was quite a shock when her daughter was born and she felt disappointment and fear. She asked God why and wondered how in the world she would be able to deal with it. Would they be able to handle the extra expense of any special care that would be needed? How in the world would they know what care was needed and how to access it? Who could help?

Megan said their daughter's birth started them on a journey that changed their life. Their church family surrounded them. Other moms contacted her, letting her know that their children had special needs too and they connected them with agencies and services that could help. Megan said what started as a very lonely experience has ended up being a journey of God's incredible provision. She has an incredible network of moms who support her. She no longer looks at Down's syndrome as a disability but as a part of her daughter's life that makes her uniquely precious. She said she can't imagine their life without her.

Are you a mom facing a difficult health situation with your child? Realize now that you are not alone. There are a myriad of organizations set up to help you. Start with your church or neighborhood school and talk to another mom who can help.

What About My Child's Spiritual Growth?

An additional worry that moms alluded to was related to the spiritual growth of their child. How can you as a mom help your child in their decision to follow Christ? What if they don't want to go to church with you or don't seem interested in God at all? Terri, a mom of three, shared this: "This is something I worry about that I feel like I have no control over. I know my kids have to make the decision to follow Christ for themselves. The only thing I know to do is pray and talk to them about what my relationship with Christ means to me."

Terri is right. She can't control this, but as a mom she is a powerful influence. In the book *Sticky Faith*, a quote by Robyn points out how powerful the influence of a mom and dad is: "My parents are probably the biggest influence out of anybody."[14]

Moms, your conversations and prayers make a difference. Talk to your children about God. Find a great church where your children can hear about how much God loves them. Let them see you pray and take time to pray with them. According to Barna Research, the greatest window of opportunity is when a child is in the preteen years and the most effective methods are talking to your children about God and daily modeling your own Christian walk.[15] How you live and what you say matters.

SERENITY NOW

So here's the reality about our mom fears. There are dangers out there to be afraid of. Bad things can happen. But just as the Serenity Prayer says:

God, grant me the serenity to accept the things I cannot change,

The courage to change the things I can,
And wisdom to know the difference.

And that is my prayer for you and for me. That we will focus on what we can do for our children and not let our fears about "what if" carry us away. And as we do, that God may fill us with his wisdom and his peace. So what could this look like in your life? What if you are overcome by fear right now as you read this? What if you are experiencing something that is very real and is keeping you up at night? I understand. I've been there. Let me share a couple of ways I combat my own fear:

I let God's Word comfort me. Even in the midst of my fear, I recite passages like Psalm 56:3, "When I am afraid, I put my trust in you." It reminds me that even when I am overcome with fear, I can call out to God and he hears me. He's not just watching me from afar, but he's right there with me.

I get honest with God. I pray. I call out to him when I'm scared and I let him know how I'm feeling. Then I get quiet and give him time to quiet my heart.

I lean into others. I don't know about you, but when I'm really afraid, I don't like to be alone. It helps to put words to my fears and share them with others who have dealt with fear themselves.

Take a minute and reflect on the questions below and give God a few minutes to speak to you.

Let's Get Practical

1. Do you resonate with the top five parenting fears, or are there others that strike your heart? Where do you think they come from?
2. Think about the strategy of "taking a vacation from your fears" by focusing on the precautions you can take to minimize risk and giving yourself permission to think about the positive. Which of these strategies works better for you in getting your fear under control? Is there another strategy that you utilize when fearful thoughts strike?
3. What do you think God is trying to say to you through this chapter?

Let's Take Action

Choose a Bible verse or a truth that helps you focus your thoughts on the positive (such as Philippians 4:8 or the truth that most of what we worry about never happens). Write it down and keep it near to read when fear hits.

4

THERE IS NO PERFECT CHILD

I remember looking at my beautiful, brilliant daughter and wondering, *Who in the world is this child?* Ridiculous thought, isn't it? Of course she was mine and I loved her fiercely. But if this uncomfortable thought has ever flitted across your brain, you are not alone. Most mothers have felt a mixture of surprise, pride, and sometimes dismay as they've watched their children develop unique parts of their personalities or pursue interests very different from their own.

Most mothers do love their children and are tremendously proud of them. But you probably have worried about your child becoming their own person and being different than you. Going even deeper, what if you and your child don't have much in common when it comes to interests or hobbies? What if your child's personality rubs against yours and sparks conflict? What if your offspring has the personality of your aunt Jane, who was the one you never really got along with? Could there be raw moments when you wonder if you even *like* that adorable child that you love so much? Elizabeth, a mom of two, shared this exact thought.

A Challenging Child: Elizabeth's Story

In the early morning hours my sleepy daughter crawls into bed and curls up next to me—stealing my pillow, taking up a good portion of our king-sized bed with her small frame, throwing her tiny foot on top of me, and warming my heart with her need for closeness.

"Mama, I'm hungry."

"It's not quite time to get up yet, love. We need a little more rest, then I'll go downstairs to get you breakfast."

"But I want lemonade."

"I understand. Let's snuggle for a little while and we'll go downstairs soon."

"No. I said I want lemonade *now*. And if you don't get me some lemonade *right this instant* I am going to kick you."

And so she does—in the face. Nothing says "I love you, Mommy" quite like a kick in the face at six in the morning. I think, *I love you, but I'm not sure I like you.* This is not what I expected motherhood to look like.

I envisioned parenting to be a golden-rule type of scenario. I was a self-motivated child, working hard because it was the right thing to do, loving and respecting my parents, and receiving love and respect in return. I didn't grow up in a picture-perfect wonderland of family life—we had our challenges, like any family. But I envisioned my future children to be thoughtful, intellectual, and for the most part, obedient—once they were done with the diapers and drool stage, of course. I expected that most of the challenges of motherhood would be internal—figuring out what to do with an infant (I never did take to babysitting as a kid), deciding when and how to implement allowance and chore time, ensuring that my kids were presented with nutritious foods and encouraged to make good choices. Somewhere along the way I forgot to remember that children are born with more than physical needs—they have a personality, quirks, and expectations all their own.

My daughter has an expansive vocabulary, and as an avid reader and sometime writer, I am thrilled that she treasures words and stores them up, just like her mama does. But I do have a least favorite word, and as chance would have it, my daughter found it. From the backseat of the car, just past her second birthday, my darling, inquisitive, intelligent two-year-old proved herself a force to be reckoned with. "I *hate* you!" And those four little letters broke my mommy heart in an instant. "She doesn't even understand what that means," said her father. "I remember the first time your younger sister said that to me," said my own mother. "Of course she doesn't mean it," said a friend. And I relearned a vital truth I thought I knew—this time from the perspective of parenthood: Words can hurt.

Two years of waiting for the miracle of conception,

ten years of marriage to my high school sweetheart and best friend, and finally—*finally*—we had a baby girl of our own. But from the time she arrived as a squalling, colicky infant to the vehemence with which she demands to be in charge of most aspects of her daily life to the challenges that occur on a weekly basis in her kindergarten classroom—I have been blessed with a strong-willed child whom I love, and marvel at, and cry over, and sometimes just don't know what to do with. And nothing about motherhood or the relationship I share with my daughter is what I expected.

I've read books, taken classes with my husband, prayed, blamed myself, shaken my head, laughed, cried, eaten ice cream, consulted friends and mentors, and wondered silently, and even aloud, whether I am capable of parenting the force-of-nature that is my firstborn child. Sometimes she yells. She refuses to follow my directions. She throws things at her bedroom door during timeout. She physically lashes out.

She is beautifully and wonderfully made—of that I am certain. When she doesn't know I'm listening, she comforts her younger brother (he is three, she has just turned five) and even shares her toys. She loves to craft homemade cards for friends and family. She can't wait for me to finish eating dinner so she can crawl into my lap for a snuggle. Other times I long for a little r-e-s-p-e-c-t, or even just a little cooperation—but we do love each other.

I survive being the mother of a challenging child, with a personality and temperament not at all like mine, by realizing (and this is an ongoing process) that there is no perfect picture of what being a mom is. Many times as a mother I am muddling through, praying, hoping, not always confident in my parenting, but I keep on going. I don't always like my daughter's choices or behavior, but my love for her is strong enough to remind me to look for the beautiful in the midst of the difficult. I work on letting go of former expectations—and many times throwing all of my expectations out the window and just letting it be. And I hang on to the notion that she is created for a marvelous purpose—something beyond my limited mom vision—that requires her unique strength, intellect, and even her stubbornness. I can't wait to see what God has in store for her. ❋

Letting Expectations Go

As Elizabeth candidly shared, being a mom isn't living a fairy tale of perfect mothering with perfect children. We can have all sorts of expectations of what parenthood will be like, but our hopes and expectations will not change how our children behave or how they react to us.

As I've talked with other moms, I've realized I'm not alone in creating an idyllic portrait of mommyhood. We picture the fun and excitement of sharing the things we love with our children and expect them to love the same things. We anticipate they will have unique personalities but ones that are similar to our own. If, as children, we were quiet, obedient rule followers, we might expect our daughter will be one too. If we love meeting people and being the life of the party, why wouldn't our child be the same way? But when vastly different temperaments pop up in our children, we are taken by surprise. Maybe our son has a penchant for bending every rule that comes his way, or maybe our daughter is extremely shy and hates crowds. Sometimes surprising, even disturbing behaviors pop up, and the door opens to panic.

I recently talked with Alex, a mom of four, who said there have been times when her children's behavior has not only surprised or embarrassed her but struck fear in her heart. She shared the story of a recent outing at a children's museum where her beautiful daughter went from an adorable blonde toddler to a miniature version of a monster.

What Kind of Monster Are You Raising?
Alex's Story

The baby's head was perfect, round and bald as a baby's head should be. In retrospect I thought it looked like a shiny apple, which might have been part of the problem. My daughter Gabi was a year older than this unsuspecting baby, and as she innocently approached her she reached out her hand to touch the perfect round head. I felt a surge of adrenaline as I saw the look in Gabi's eye. I'd seen that look too often in recent months, in the moment right before her teeth made contact. My daughter's blue eyes locked onto the baby's perfect apple head, and before I could reach her, Gabi bent over and chomped down. I saw the horror on the baby's mother's face as she looked at my Gabi and then at me. This other woman didn't need to say a word. The expression on her face screamed, *How could she? How could YOU? What kind of monster are you raising?*

Driving home in the car, I blinked over and over to clear my eyes of the tears threatening to spill over. I needed to keep driving, to get both of us home. Home, where she couldn't hurt anyone else, where I wouldn't have to worry about the angry looks and silent, accusing questions of a rightfully horrified mom. And as I drove, my thoughts got carried away. *Why does she do this? Other kids don't. What is wrong with her? What kind of a mother am I that she continues to do this? What if this is a problem that can't be fixed? We'll never be able to leave the house, to be with other kids. For the safety of all the other children I'll need to keep her isolated so she doesn't hurt anyone else. And she'll probably have to go to a special school, one for delinquent children. It will probably be a private school and we already live on such a tight budget, how will we ever afford a special school? I'll have to get a job, one that makes a lot of money. And what if she never gets better?*

Within two minutes I determined what my life would look like for the next twenty years, including visiting Gabi in a juvenile detention center. Gabi, in her required orange jumpsuit that loudly proclaimed *this child bites.* I, looking haggard and dejected, leaning on my equally devastated husband, wondering what else we could have done to help her.

Later that day, in the middle of a phone conversation with an older mom friend, I relayed the disturbing biting incident. Her gentle laugh and words of understanding changed my perspective. Her daughter, now a teenager, had also been a pint-sized aggressor. I knew this young lady. She was the one who helped in Sunday school and was a poised, healthy, well-adjusted teen. I felt my shoulders relax. She was kind. She didn't hit or bite strangers. She was college bound and seemed to have genuine friendships. Maybe this *was* just a phase. Maybe Gabi *would* outgrow this biting fixation, and special schools were not in our future.

I hung up relieved and grateful that this woman

didn't ridicule me for my fears. She didn't shame me for having a daughter who couldn't keep her teeth to herself or scold me for blowing it out of proportion. She simply shared her own experiences and let me know I was not alone. ✿

WAIT TO WORRY

Can you hear the "me too" all over that story? So many of us have been there, wondering if *our* precious baby will grow up into someone no one else will like, someone *we* don't even like. Isn't it interesting how our thoughts as moms can carry us to a scary, blown-out-of-proportion place when really all we are dealing with is typical childhood behavior? Alex experienced behavior from her daughter that took her by surprise, and she was wise to get help with her perspective by letting an experienced mom talk her down from the ledge of impending juvenile incarceration. By ourselves, it is easy to look at the behavior happening in the moment and forecast the future, letting our mom fears carry us away. It's tempting to jump to the conclusion that there's something seriously wrong with our child and begin to wonder if we are to blame. In reality Gabi didn't have a serious behavior problem. Although Gabi was exhibiting behavior that needed to be dealt with, it didn't make her a bad child, nor did it make Alex a bad mom.

When our daughter Brittainy was four, we began to notice a pattern of shyness. Since my husband was a pastor, everyone at the church knew our kids' names and talked with them freely.

This didn't seem to bother our son, who was easy with people, even those he didn't know well. But Brittainy's personality was different. She seemed to hang back, watching people from a distance, often standing behind me. When people would say hello to her, she sometimes looked down and waited for me to speak for her. When this happened I felt pressured to prompt Brittainy to answer politely and I would feel irritation boil up within me. *I've taught her to look people in the eye and give a response. Why is she acting this way?*

I'll never forget the day we were at her grandparent's house, introducing her to an aunt and uncle and others she had not yet met. She was hiding behind me, with her face hidden in my skirt. I pulled her out and with my arm around her, encouraged her with the words, "Brittainy, say hello to the people." I wanted to sink into the floor when I heard her mumble loud enough for everyone to hear, "But I hate the people!"

I remember having moments of despair thinking that I was raising an antisocial child, who would grow up without any close friends, unhappy and alone. An older and wiser mom friend gently let me off the hook by urging me to relax and give Brittainy a chance to figure out her own rhythm with people. In essence, she was telling me to *wait to worry*. She said Brittainy was learning who she was and how she felt comfortable interacting with people. As a mom it was my job to teach her respect and love and kindness and help her develop the interpersonal tools to do this. But it was also my job as a mom to watch, wait, and learn who Brittainy was becoming.

Wait to worry is such a great concept. There may be serious issues down the road, but why conjure them up before you know there is really anything serious to face? Pause. Give calm reflection. Learn. And wait to see what will unfold.

MY CHILD IS NOT ME

As Brittainy got older we could see she was a talented athlete. She loved basketball and soccer and anything that allowed her to play outdoors in her basketball shorts and tennis shoes. She would spend hours out on the driveway perfecting her free throws and three pointers. Sometimes she wore her soccer shin guards long after practice was over. She saw absolutely no reason to ever wear a dress. She considered glittery nail polish and hair accessories beyond ponytail holders things to be avoided. In her opinion, sweat was the evidence that fun was being had, and you hadn't really had any fun until you were covered in it.

Compare that to her mom (that would be me). I grunt when I shoot a free throw. I tend to fall down when I run (and even when I don't — see opening story!). I have never donned a pair of shin guards out of fear they would surely make my legs look fat. When I was in college I took tennis as my physical education credit so I could wear a cute skirt. I avoided sweating whenever possible (I like to refer to it as glistening), and I'm much happier on the bench watching a sport than playing it.

This became an issue.

Since Brittainy was a sports lover, she and her dad and older brother often talked basketball over dinner. The three of them would head out the door and shoot baskets after the meal was over, while I watched from the sidelines holding my mug of coffee. It was fun to see the three of them having fun together, but it began to make me wonder about what Brittainy and I had in common. More often, our points of polarization began to surface. We didn't agree on how she should wear her hair. She detested the clothes I suggested and said everything I bought her itched. I loved to browse in shops and look at shoes and clothes, necklaces and earrings. She thought this so very boring.

To bridge the gap, I decided to plan some mother-daughter dates so we could spend more time together. I started by asking Brittainy what she would like to do.

"We could go over to the field and play soccer."

I'll have to admit this suggestion didn't fill me with joy. Running, sweating, and chasing a ball around didn't sound like a good time to me, but I was all in if it meant spending time with my daughter. For our first outing, we did plan an afternoon on a field near our house, but it didn't last long. I had no skills. I was slow. Brittainy wanted to teach me how to do a bicycle kick. I wondered what bicycles had to do with soccer. She wanted to practice blocking balls at the goal, but I kicked the ball so slow my grandma could have beaten it to the goalie box. She wanted to practice scoring, so we switched places, with me as goalie. She had to tell me more than once to not duck from the ball.

But we were determined. We planned another night to go get ice cream at the mall. As we leisurely walked by the stores savoring our cones, we passed a fun jewelry store aimed at young girls. We wandered in. There were so many fun things to look at, hats, purses, sparkly tights, and headbands. I suggested a few necklaces I thought Brittainy might like. *No thanks.* We looked at earrings and I asked Brittainy if she would like to get her ears pierced. *No.* We wandered back out.

On the way home in the car I began to have a niggling fear. What if Brittainy and I had nothing in common? What if she didn't like spending time with me? I heard other moms talk about wonderful mom-daughter nights working on fun projects together or trying out new hairstyles and painting each other's nails. Was I such a sorry mom that I couldn't find common ground with my daughter? Did this make me a bad mom?

When Brittainy was born, I had dreamed of doing girly things together. Days of giggles and cookie making and talking about things only moms and daughters talk about. As we drove home from our mall date, I began to wonder if I had conjured up a fairy-tale picture of motherhood. And it didn't account for a child who had a very different personality than mine.

On the way home from our second less-than-perfect mom and daughter night, I asked Brittainy how she felt about our time together. With perfect nine-year-old straightforwardness she said bluntly, "It wasn't much fun. You like looking at hair stuff, but I'm not you."

Today Is Just a Snapshot

Brittainy was so right — she wasn't me. This was a good thing. How many slow, nonathletic shoe shoppers did the world need?

Her personality was — and still is — different than mine. Her shyness has turned into a beautiful part of her personality that manifests itself in select, deep relationships. Her love for sports and athleticism is part of her zest for life and commitment to hard work and excellence. The moments I wasted on fears and worries that she and I would never find common ground or get along were truly wasted ones.

Brittainy and I have found we both love some of the same movies — anything featuring a snarky Meryl Streep performance gets us going. We've seen *The Devil Wears Prada* together more than once; it's worth it for the shoes alone! We have found things we both love to shop for, like fashion forward tops (she makes sure I don't go for any "old lady" picks) and steals at Goodwill. Brittainy taught me that a keen eye and a little patience can yield thrifty results, and we love to celebrate an especially chic find at the ice cream shop. She loves music and so do I. We both always notice adorable little children with chubby cheeks. I look at her today and remember the frustrating moments of fear, wondering who she would become, and now I wonder why I wasted energy on worry.

I know what it feels like to watch your child in the midst of a terrible tantrum and see flashes of a person you don't like. I have found it impossible to be patient through their hatefulness or rebellion, and have wondered, *what kind of a monster am I raising?* But my friend and mentor, Reggie Joiner, CEO of ReThink (an organization that specializes in helping parents navigate the parenting path), has helped me realize that many times as parents what we worry about is just a snapshot, a temporary picture of *this day alone*. Like Instagram, these snapshots of parenthood capture what your child looks like in this moment, with that crooked smile and patch of hair that sticks up in the back. It is a picture of their *current* tantrums and personality struggles and behavior issues. No single snapshot can convey who your child will *become* — the complete, complex album of a life which reveals God's good plan for her. It is *this* creation — this *series* of life portraits of your child — which will endure, not the frustrating snapshot moments. God's album for your child gives the big picture of lessons learned, of temperaments refined, of maturity blending with experience to produce a beautiful person indeed.

Moms, while it is so tempting to base our fears on the snapshots of today, it's much healthier to ground our hopes on the rich album of portraits your child is growing into.

THERE IS NO PERFECT

Here's what it has taken me a lifetime to learn: There is no perfect child. Children kick and scream and bite. They talk back. They poop their pants at the most inconvenient moments. They embarrass us in front of strangers and family and make us wonder if they will ever be normal at all. They make us want to run from the room screaming, and we wonder if we even want them in our house. But it's a perfect match, because there aren't any perfect moms either. We lose our temper and embarrass ourselves. We nag. We worry. We let our fears get away from us and waste precious moments worrying about things that will never be.

Recently, God has been taking my thoughts to Psalm 23, reminding me that God is my shepherd. He will lead me to green pastures, where I will find everything I need. He will lead me beside still waters, where he will calm my anxious mom heart. He will restore my soul with the exact peace and rest I need.

Oh God, calm my heart with the still waters of your quiet love. Restore my soul from painful worry and help me to rest in the fact that you've got my back.

Moms, I'm just now learning to relax and to wait to worry. It's my prayer that as we continue through this book, you will too.

LET'S GET PRACTICAL

1. Is there something about your child that embarrasses you and makes you wonder if you're a good mom? What is it?
2. Have you ever dealt with thoughts of not liking your child's behavior or personality? What did you do about it?
3. Is it easy or hard for you to picture the *portrait of tomorrow* when it comes to your child? Why do you think this is?

LET'S TAKE ACTION

Do you have a "panic go-to person"? Someone who remains ever calm and can talk you down off the ledge of unreasonable fear? Look around and see if you can find one.

5

WILL HAVING A BABY CHANGE MY LIFE FOREVER?

The answer of course is yes. How could pushing a baby out through your body not change you forever? But if this question resonates with fear in your heart about how you will deal with these lasting changes, and perhaps even strikes a chord of terror, you are not alone.

What is it about reproduction that is inherently fear inducing?

For many of us it is fear of the unknown that plagues us. We are skillful at thinking up all of the worst-case scenarios, envisioning ourselves completely undone or unable to cope, with a stretched-out uterus and never getting a wink of sleep *for the rest of our lives*. With everyone talking about how a baby not only wrecks your body, but totally turns your life upside down, who can blame us for feeling overwhelmed at the very thought of embarking on such a life-changing journey?

My own fears centered on two things, my comfortable life and my body. As for my life, just how much comfort was I going to have to give up? Would I still have time for friends, for fun, for an occasional quiet coffee at Starbucks? How would this change my relationship with Geoff? What about sex? Was this gone forever? Would I ever get my body back? I had seen the big belly pictures in the pregnancy books. I didn't know skin could stretch that much and I had my doubts as to where it would all go after the baby came.

If you've ever wondered thoughts like these and then wondered if you were completely selfish and self-absorbed, you are in good company. It's normal to worry about how things will change. And no, this doesn't make you a bad person or a bad mom. As we prepared for this book, we asked lots of questions, and as moms candidly shared their stories with us, we began to see that the fear about how your life will change and how you will be able to adapt to it is very real. Mandy, a mom of three, shares her story of coming to terms with motherhood.

What Happened to My Life? Mandy's Story

The water grew colder with each passing minute, but I couldn't pry myself off of the shower floor. Waiting for me on the bathroom counter was a towel, my favorite ugly pajamas, and a positive pregnancy test. Two hours earlier I had unwrapped the test fully believing that this was just a false alarm, that there was no way that I could possibly be pregnant. We had only been married for a year, I was barely out of college, and I had plans for my life. So when the little blue plus sign made an appearance I alternated between staring at the test in my shaking hand and staring at myself in the bathroom mirror. And because I had no clue what else to do—I prayed. I prayed the only way I know how to pray—in moans and accusations and tears and wild promises. *I am in no way qualified to be a mom. I am the last person that should be raising another human being. I am selfish and determined and I don't want my body to be ruined.* And yes, I talk to God this way. He gets me and isn't at all worried that sometimes I exaggerate and say things I don't mean.

When I finally stood up from the shower floor, shivering more from fear than the cold water, I made a decision. I decided to become a mom.

For each of us our journey toward motherhood is so different. When I was a teenager I struggled with an eating disorder that left me with a lingering concern that I had messed up my body so much that I wouldn't be able to conceive a baby. I have other friends who took birth control pills to prevent pregnancy only to find out that it was never going to happen anyway. Other friends adopted babies, choosing to stand in the gap for women who couldn't raise them alone. No matter what our path looks like, there are no shortcuts toward motherhood. It's as if God knows we all need time to prepare. Whether you labored to push a baby from your body or labored with paperwork and red tape to bring a baby into your family, the process of becoming a mom is a journey. And so often the journey is accompanied by fear.

When my first baby Joseph was born, my whole family was in the room to experience the event. It was a long process that ended with a near C-section and my new best friend, the forceps. It was quite a crowd who endured the delivery with me: my mom, grandma, in-laws, and my brother (who may be forever scarred after witnessing such an event). For some reason it was deeply comforting to know that the newest member of our tribe was being welcomed into the world by a family that was willing to endure blood and guts to witness his arrival. Becoming a mom makes us deeply vulnerable. We share our insides, our most private parts, and then expose those parts to the world. Our souls become raw with the beauty and pain of bringing a child into the world.

Looking back on the first year of being a mom, I have to admit that if I had known that my life would be sliced open so entirely, I would never have had the courage to make the decision I did on that shower floor. From the moment I pushed a baby out of my body, I was never the same. My old life that I thought was so beautiful was ruined entirely. My new life, which included a dizzying amount of schedules, routines, and details, was so much more beautiful than anything I had thought I wanted. My life that I wept tears at the thought of losing was a mere sketch of the masterpiece that awaited me. Some things were lost, but nothing is missing. Motherhood and the

gifts that accompany it have become the most wondrous gifts I have ever received. ✹

REAL QUESTIONS

Maybe you can relate to Mandy, with her overwhelming fear of
what becoming a mom would mean in her life. Perhaps you still
have questions about what to expect as a mom. In my life I've
found it immensely helpful to talk my questions and fears over
with other moms who understand and have wisdom to share.
Here are a few of the honest questions we know moms are asking
and some of the insights that we've gathered from some of the
smartest moms we know. We've even included a practical step to
help you get started.

Will I lose my identity?

Going from nonparent to parent is arguably one of the most
significant shifts in identity that any person can go through. I
remember having a breakdown just a few days after bringing
Michael home from the hospital. I was exhausted. I was worried
I couldn't do this. The question that I couldn't shake from my
mind was *What have I gotten myself into?*

What I didn't know at the time was that this moment of panic
hits every new mom at some point, whether it is the moment you
see the positive pregnancy test or when you've nursed a newborn nonstop for what seems like years. It's the moment when
we realize how much change we've experienced and are forced

to wrestle to the ground what it means for our future. For me, questions began to hit from all sides. *Will I ever get to have an adult conversation? Is this seriously what my body is going to look like? Will I be worrying nonstop for the rest of my life? Will I ever have the energy to pursue the things I love?*

The process of becoming you is a lifelong pursuit. It's the nature of a mom to sacrifice, but good moms don't have to be martyrs to motherhood. The healthiest and happiest moms I know are the ones who see motherhood as a complement to their identity instead of the focal point. Having a baby is a key that unlocks a new piece of yourself and is an opportunity to uncover a whole new layer of your identity that you would never have experienced otherwise. Being a mom reveals and refines the less savory parts of our personalities and adds depth to the already beautiful parts. When we decide to wade into this uncharted territory, we are able to realize that we are becoming more of ourselves through the process of becoming a mom.

To try: Do a self-assessment asking yourself two questions: (1) How intentional am I about taking care of my emotional needs? (2) What is one thing I can do this week that will make me feel energized?

Will having a baby change my relationship with my husband?

Let's be honest. Yes. I can tell you that almost everything about my relationship with Geoff changed when we had a baby. Not only were we partners and lovers, but now we were also parents.

Our love was made tangible in the form of a tiny human who was needy and perfect in every possible way. And that infant gave a purpose to our lives that we had never experienced before. Something profound happens when your lives are knit together by flesh and bone and breath.

Mandy adds that bringing a baby into the world makes you feel like a complete family. "I remember bringing Joseph home from the hospital and having Joe look over at me as he said, 'This feels right,' like somehow we weren't complete until Joseph joined us. And the same thing happened with Ellie and Charlotte as well. With each baby that joined our family we felt more whole. Like a missing puzzle piece that we didn't even know was missing. We became better with each addition. Joe and I have bonded over our shared life experiences. He has never been as sexy to me as when he gets up in the middle of the night in order to let me sleep a little longer. And sometimes, on those maddening nights when the kids' bedtime routine feels like a game of whack-a-mole, we joke that we are war buddies. We have secrets and inside jokes that only we know, all because we share a love for three little people who sometimes leave us feeling like prisoners of war in our own home. We have lived through the best and worst together, and we are better partners because of it."

Adding a baby makes it challenging to keep your relationship a top priority. At first it may feel like you are navigating new waters and barely keeping yourselves afloat. You'll feel consumed with your baby, and if you are like most moms, there will be times when it will feel like your hubby is requiring as much care as your newborn. The trick to keeping your relationship healthy is to make time for one another. For us it meant making regular date nights a priority. I am a believer that date nights are the best therapy money can buy. They reminded me of who I was, who we were, before the baby arrived. They reminded me that experiencing life without kids from time to time is essential, and that we're more than just parents. This is easy to forget, especially when you have an all-consuming baby to care for.

To try: Plan a date night for you and your husband. Don't be discouraged if one or both of you is not excited about the idea up front, but just try to relax and get back in touch with who you were before baby arrived. Spend some quality time talking about anything but your kids.

Will my sex life ever be the same?

After the tremendous changes that happen in your body during pregnancy, it's normal to wonder if everything will bounce back to its pre-pregnancy form, including your sexual desire. Rest assured, it will (mostly), but your sex "want to" may take awhile to catch up. I've been told that after having a baby you are hormonally conditioned to be more interested in your baby than your husband for the first few months. It is a natural process that ensures human survival. And let's face it, you are exhausted. It is totally natural for it to take awhile to feel like yourself again. As moms we spend so much time giving to our babies that sometimes we don't have any energy left for anything else. Give yourself time. Don't beat yourself up or hold yourself to unrealistic expectations.

One thing that I had to learn the hard way was to remember my husband's feelings through the whole experience. Bringing a baby into the world can be just as stressful for our guys, as they now shoulder the responsibility of a bigger family. Just as we have to wrestle with what becoming a mom means, so it is for the dads. They are facing big adjustments as well, and just because we have the babies doesn't mean we have the right to be insensitive about our husbands' needs. For most men, sex is an important part of expressing love, which means that we need to make an effort to make sure they don't feel like we have forgotten them. Making sure that sex is a life-giving part of your relationship will take some energy, but it will be worth the effort and will help to let your man know that he is still a priority.

To try: Not in the mood? Get your mind in gear by helping yourself relax before your husband gets home. Take a hot bath or a rest while the kids nap. Send your hubby a suggestive text. It will give him something to think about all day while he is at work and will surely help to spice things up when he gets home.

Will I lose the baby weight?

The good news is yes, you probably will. The bad news is that you are not going to walk out of the hospital in your skinny jeans.

Here is what no one told me: You will leave the hospital with a belly that looks like you are still pregnant. I will never forget walking down the driveway to get the mail from our mailbox and a well-meaning neighbor calling over, "When is your baby due?" Mike had arrived the week before! It's wise to not stress about it and instead put your focus on taking care of yourself. It took nine months to build a baby and put the weight on. Give yourself a little grace and allow the same amount of time to take it off.

Well-intentioned friends may warn you that having a baby will "ruin" your body. They will warn you your breasts will never be the same and your belly button will forever be unrecognizable. It's amazing to me why women share these details because they are certainly not helpful. Instead of standing in solidarity with our body, we are told to face off against it, unable to be totally content until we look like we did before we had a baby. We need to reframe our expectations. Your body will not be ruined. It will perform tasks that you never thought were physically possible. It will nourish and push life into the world. At the end of the process things may look a little different, and that is good. It means we have done something important.

To try: A great way to help feel more like yourself is to do something physical that you enjoy. Don't try to put yourself on a rigorous exercise regimen or set impossible goals. Focus on some physical movement that you enjoy, like dancing or just walking.

Will my friendships change?

The honest truth is some of your friends will be excited and happy to come by and hold the baby, while others won't. They may drop out for a while, but that's okay. Everyone handles change differently. Your job as a mom is to take care of your little one, and it is vitally important that you also take care of yourself.

This includes seeking friendships that enrich and support you in this stage of your life.

Maybe you used to be in a book club with a fun group of women, or you and your husband might have been in a young couples group before baby arrived, but now you don't have the energy to make it to these meetings. The key to building a fun group of mom friends is to recognize that moms in your same stage of life likely have similar schedules, constraints, and even the same lack of sleep! Even the introverts among us can bond over the common ground of motherhood.

To try: Find a moms group! MOPS is a great place to meet up with moms who understand what your days are like, and want some of the same things you do — a break, an uninterrupted bite to eat, a chance to chat — a *shower*. Another option is to show up where the moms are — the park, playland, Starbucks. Put on your mom badge of courage and invite another mom into conversation by complimenting her darling baby — then see where things go. Chances are this mom needs a friend too.

Will I ever sleep again?

This is the million dollar question! For the first few months you may feel like you are living in a sleepless haze. The most down-to-earth mom advice is to just go with it. Sleep when your baby sleeps and don't stress out about not having a set schedule yet. A key to this is to give yourself permission to let the laundry, dishes, and housework go in lieu of an opportune time to rest. Eventually your baby will sleep through the night — and so will you. Lean into wise mom friends who have traveled this road and keep perspective by remembering that each stage, including the not-enough-sleep stage, isn't your forever reality.

To try: Set up a nap swap with a friend. Take her baby for a few hours so that she can have a few hours of uninterrupted sleep. Then swap with her so you can do the same. Two hours of uninterrupted sleep can make a big difference.

How will I find the energy to do it all?

You won't. End of story. A while back I got some sage advice from an older mom who said, "Just because you can do anything doesn't mean you should do everything." How true. Don't expect yourself to be able to accomplish more than is humanly possible. Choose what is most important to tackle and then leave the rest for another day. This early stage of parenting is time consuming and exhausting. Give yourself permission to not have to do it all in one day. Take your eyes off of that other mom who seems to get everything done and then some. Tell yourself you will do your best and your best is all you can do. And don't let Pinterest convince you otherwise.

Will other moms judge me?

The sad news is they might, but the great news is you get to choose whether or not you pay attention. It's sad that moms will pick at each other or make another mom feel like she is less than she ought to be. But I think the most damaging voice can be the one that comes from within. A mom of three shared this:

"The truth is the only mommy war I have encountered is the one that happens in my own head. I judge myself way more than any other mom judges me. I second-guess every decision I make. I judge myself for how much I work, but when I stayed home full-time, I constantly felt like I had to make excuses for why I didn't work. In my twelve years of being a mom, I have found that other moms are my biggest cheerleaders. They are the ones who encourage me to pursue my passions and to embrace the style of parenting that works best for our family. It is the other moms in my life who have given me the best advice and who have offered support when I most needed it."

To try: Focus on doing the *opposite* of judging yourself. Instead of ruminating on what you do wrong, remind yourself of what you do well as a mom.

God and Moms

When it comes to making the choice to raise children it is comforting to remember that God "gets" mothering. He wrapped his divinity in a baby blanket and entrusted it to a teenage mom who had no resources. This tells me that God has infinite confidence in us, which means that we can take the next steps without fear.

We are allowed to be afraid, especially when we are facing a new challenge that we have no experience with. In these situations we get to practice being courageous, developing resilience and moral muscle. Courage doesn't mean we're not afraid anymore; it just means our actions aren't controlled by our fears.

The beauty is that God won't invite us anywhere God's not already waiting.

LET'S GET PRACTICAL

1. What was your own journey toward motherhood like? What new fears and questions has it raised?
2. Think about times in the past when you faced a situation where you didn't know what to expect. What happened? How did you navigate the uncertainty? Did you learn anything from that experience?
3. What is your greatest need today? Is it quality friend time, quiet time to reflect and rebalance, or something else? What will you do about it?

LET'S TAKE ACTION

Find another mom to encourage. Think about what you would like someone to tell you as a mom. Be specific in your comments and aim them at things you've noticed about that mom (i.e., I saw you with your daughter the other day and I love the way you encouraged her. You are such a good mom!). If there isn't a mom nearby you are ready to give a shout out to, call or email your sister, cousin, or college roommate to pass on some mom encouragement. It'll make her day and giving encouragement away will give you a lift as well.

6

FEAR OF WHAT'S AHEAD: TEENAGERS

We were young, me and this youth pastor husband of mine. We had only been married a month and here we were in Houston, Texas, far away from my hometown of St. Louis, Missouri, and responsible for the middle and high school students at our church. We were hoping to have children of our own someday, so I began to get to know the teens in our group with a bit of awe and wonder and sometimes amusement. They were smart and funny and creative. They were loud and messy. Sometimes they showed enthusiasm and delight and laughed with abandon like little kids. Other times they carried themselves with sophisticated airs of disdain and seemed older than their years. They had opinions of their own which they stated arrogantly, seeming so sure of themselves. Other times they fumbled along, not seeming sure of anything at all. As I listened to their stories I found myself wondering, *I wonder if their mom knows they are doing that.*

As it turned out, many times their moms *didn't* know they were doing that.

Even before our kids were thoughts in our minds, I began to fear having teenagers. Good Lord, what if our son is loud and obnoxious like *him*? What will we do if our daughter is an emotional roller coaster like *her*? How will we help them navigate peer pressure and making the right decisions about drugs and sex and oh good grief, *they will want to get their driver's license!* I began to wonder if we just shouldn't stick with having a dog.

I'll never forget a heartbreaking conversation with a mom who shared some of the things her fifteen-year-old daughter was going through. She was having trouble in school and the mom was getting called frequently to come in and talk with the principal. They suspected she was sneaking out at night, and they watched with horror as she chose friends that they knew would lead to trouble. My young, inexperienced heart didn't know what to say. I listened, we prayed, I connected her with some other moms of teenage girls, but after the conversation I walked away thinking that being a dog owner was looking better and better.

But as I got to know some of the families and watched the way the moms and dads interacted with their teenagers, I noticed that indeed, some of them were enjoying their kids and having fun. The teenagers were an integral part of the family. They talked to each other about their lives and seemed not just like parent and child, but people who actually liked to hang out with each other. They yelled, had fights, slammed doors, and called each other names, but at the end of the day, they loved each other. I began to have hope.

In an online article called "10 Things I Love about My Teen," Diana Landon says, "Teenagers are supposed to be awful. Like werewolves, they transform overnight into hairy monsters. They hate you, they defy you, and they make your life miserable. Oddly, I am enjoying having a teenager so far. Sure, there are problems with missing homework, he calls me a hypocrite and I doubt he tells me everything. But there are also plenty of things to love about my teen."[16] She went on to say that her son does things around the house, like fixing the kitchen cabinets and inventing his own version of stir fried noodles that have become a family favorite. He talks about interesting things like how the American press isn't covering the attacks in Kyrgyzstan, and he even designed a miniature-sized balsa wood motorized boat for his dad to play with.

I found the extremes of that quote very interesting. "They make your life miserable.... I am enjoying having a teenager." But as I talked with other parents of teenagers, I heard similar stories. Jan, a mom of two, told me that as her oldest son began to approach the teen years, she started to worry. She would wake up in the middle of the night and begin to imagine all sorts of scenarios, from her son sleeping with his girlfriend (that he didn't have yet) to terrible family fights where their son would storm out of the house (this did actually happen). She said that they have definitely had rough days (even months), but now that both boys are teenagers she has realized it seemed much scarier than it turned out to be. She said she has found parts of their teen years she loves. She can now hold adult conversations with her boys. They talk about music and sports and why teachers don't get paid more. While she often doesn't agree with their opinions, she finds their perspectives interesting and they've had spicy family discussions (sometimes debates) that have given her new perspective. She says she loves watching the first signs of their adult personalities and delights in watching them change from little boys to almost men. Then she said some words I thought were pretty profound: "I wish I would have learned earlier to relax. I started their teen years dreading the worst. Instead I wish I would have started with a little more anticipation and wonder and a little less crazy-mama fear."

Come Down Off the Crazy Ledge

Couldn't we all do with a little less crazy-mama fear? And what great words, "anticipation and wonder." It made me begin to dream about the effect these two words could have on our mom heart. What if instead of worrying about the horrible things that *could* happen, we began to anticipate the great things that *were likely* to happen? For instance, it's almost a surety that your son will develop some interests like basketball or tinkering with cars or playing a guitar. What if you anticipated the joy it will bring you as you watch your son discover his talent and passion? Imagine the first time your daughter discovers her giftedness in soccer or singing or first begins to believe in herself as a leader? Whatever your child becomes, what if we as moms began to anticipate the becoming with a sense of wonder instead of fear? It's possible that they will make bad choices. It's probable that they will sometimes have a surly attitude. And it's even likely that they will do things that will make us lose sleep and feel like we don't have any answers at all. But it's just as possible and probable and likely that they will do things that thrill our hearts and make us so proud that tears well up and we can't believe that they are ours.

I love Jan's words "I wish I would have learned earlier to relax." Me too. When our son Mike was just entering fifth grade, we moved to South Carolina. In the school district, fifth grade was still considered part of elementary school, but at our church, he was now part of the middle school youth group. Gulp. He would be rubbing shoulders with sixth and seventh graders. I began to imagine all sorts of conversations about the boy-crazed sixth-grade girls and who-knows-what from the seventh-grade boys.

When Mike began to talk about an overnight trip that the group would be taking to nearby Myrtle Beach, I began to search for reasons he couldn't go. He could get lost from the group and they would find him wandering the streets of Myrtle Beach. He could get abducted by a motorcycle gang, never to be heard from again (motorcycles were big in Myrtle Beach and I was sure they traveled in gangs). Weren't they going swimming? He could drown in the waves, or at the very least get so horribly sunburned he would swell up like a puffer fish and be disfigured forever. As I relayed these fears to Geoff, I distinctly thought I saw *I've got a crazy mama on my hands* look in his eye, but he had the grace not to say it. He instead paused and said, "I guess he could decide to take up with a rogue motorcycle gang, but isn't it even more likely he will just have fun and make new friends?"

Come down off the crazy ledge was the message gently embedded in Geoff's words. He was right. This was a great opportunity for Mike to make friends at a new church in a new town. My worries were "what if" scenarios that weren't doing anyone any good. I could choose to let my mama fear keep Mike home where I didn't have to worry. Or, I could release the worry, acknowledging the bad possibilities but anticipating the good. My reward could then be watching with wonder as he excitedly shared details about the noisy van ride and the endless stream of nachos, slurpees, and candy that he inhaled, and the awesome beach and the kid he sat next to at McDonald's that would become a lifelong friend.

Taking a step down from the crazy ledge is a very good thing. Susan, mom of two teenage boys, shares how she deals with facing the everyday fears of raising teens.

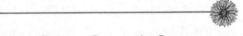

Raising Teen Boys: Susan's Story

I think, like most moms, the full effect of the "teenage boy stage times two" didn't dawn on me until I found myself knee-deep in testosterone, dirty laundry, and monosyllabic responses. One day I sort of looked up and thought—oh, this is what it's like! There are still bright spots, but I've found myself having to look beyond the daily. When your kids are young, there are lots of tangible moments of affirmation and connection. A sweet goodnight snuggle or hug and the Mother's Day handmade card extolling your good looks, loving ways, and fabulous cooking.

(Not so much on the last one for me.) As teen boys, they are finding their way, and don't have lots of time, energy, or inclination to communicate with their parents. Most of their focus goes to eating, sleeping, homework, and figuring out how to land on the next step. Then they eat some more. I have to look for the glimpses of love and connection and cherish those moments.

If you're not careful, fear and worry can become the twin peaks that dominate the mountain range that comprises raising teen boys. It can loom every morning and mock every night. I don't think my greatest fears involve the "big three" (sex, drugs, and alcohol), but rather the slow erosion of the heart issues—character, faith, and relationships. These are the path-altering choices that can dramatically skew the direction of their life. And so we try to reteach these life lessons—fearing we've forgotten something, or that they're not ready. But at some point, we just have to trust—our parenting intentions, their faith, and most importantly, God's sovereignty. And that trust empowers them. They need to know you think they can handle what's coming next.

Not too long ago, I was driving my oldest to baseball practice when I suddenly began to experience numbness on the right side of my face. It moved quickly down my body. I knew something was wrong and that I needed to pull over. Daniel had his permit, but not his license. I didn't want to scare him. I said, "Daniel, something is wrong with me, and I'm going to need to pull over." He responded very calmly, "Mom, I can drive us home and take care of you. I can handle it." In that moment, I knew that he could handle the situation before us, and so much more. Later, after I'd recovered from the atypical migraine that had caused my scary symptoms, I thanked him for being so strong. I recounted how proud I was that he had what it took to meet that challenge and that I knew, with God's help, he was ready to meet many more. He beamed. It was a great moment. Faith — 1, Fear — 0.

I will not begin to say that I have learned to keep my fear under control. It still stalks me at times and can overtake me with irrational thoughts and swirling emotions. And I have to say that I think fear is at play in my boys as well. It's much more subtle with them, and often comes out in irritability or anger. But at its heart, fear is the overdeveloped realization that we are not in control. We don't like that feeling. One way I've found to combat fear is to start my day acknowledging this fact and embracing it. My best days begin by praying aloud (so my heart and my head can hear it), "God, I'm not in control. My boys are not in control. Satan is not in control. You are in control. I am so grateful that you — the one who knows me, my hopes, and your purposes—is in charge. Help me surrender my boys to you, my will to you, and help me align my heart with yours. I trust you." When it comes to overcoming fear as a parent, there are no magic bullets, but there are three essential strategies—prayer, prayer, and more prayer. It is the sure and certain way to draw near to the only One who loves your children more than you, and can carry them all the way home.

How's That Working Out for You?

Just like Susan, I had to come to the same realization: I'm not in total control. I had heard the horror stories of kids being offered drugs at school, getting their girlfriends pregnant, driving drunk and getting into horrible accidents. As Mike approached high school, these "other kid" stories began to become very personal "my child" fears. How would I keep him safe? How would I make sure he made the right choices? How would I control the things he was exposed to and the friends he hung around? It didn't take me very long to realize I couldn't do any of those things.

What I could do *was worry.*

One day I was watching a popular psychologist on a television program as he talked to a mom who was dealing with an out-of-control daughter. She shared how miserable she was with her daughter's choices and how it was affecting her life. She was checking up on her daughter numerous times a day. She wasn't sleeping because she was watching out the window for her daughter to come home. She wasn't able to eat because her stomach hurt from worrying. She had noticed that her hair was falling out. The psychologist listened quietly and then asked a question. "And how is that working out for you?"

The mom paused, unsure of how to answer the question. She finally said, "Well, I have less hair."

The doctor had made his point. The mom's worrying wasn't doing anything but making her sick. What she wanted was for her daughter's behavior to improve. What she was doing about it was worrying and trying to control it. And her worry was having no effect on the daughter at all.

But that's the tricky part about fear and worry. Somehow we've gotten it into our heads that if we worry hard enough, if we obsess just a little bit more, if we focus with all of our strength, it will somehow prevent something horrible or turn a bad situation into something good. I have found myself working really hard on my fears, with my mind furiously covering all the possibilities, as if that, in and of itself, will keep them from happening. I don't want to be naïve, and I don't want to be caught by surprise with horrible news. But in reality, my fears and worry can't prevent bad things from happening, or turn a bad situation into something good.

Focus On the Lead Measures

I'm a goal-driven person and in my work life I get particular satisfaction from hitting my goals. I've learned though that just setting a goal with a particular number and date and then pairing that with a deep desire to hit that number and date isn't enough. I recently read a book — *The Four Disciplines of Execution* by Chris McChesney, Sean Covey, and Jim Huling — that outlines this. The authors explain that focusing on the lead measures, those things that you can influence that are predictive of your success, is far more effective than just standing back and wishing your goal into being. I found that utilizing this simple strategy relieved my angst about hitting the goal. I was actively doing the things I knew I could control. I was doing my best at them, and I could have a measure of confidence that I was focusing on what needed to be done.

How can we apply this principle to our mama fears? I learned quickly that I couldn't control Mike's friends or the choices he made or the scary things he was exposed to. Try as I might, my lying awake at night with panicky feelings about his friends and his choices and even what he was doing at that very minute wasn't changing or controlling anything. But I could control my own behavior. I could model healthy friendships and talk to him about my friends and why I chose them. I could model good choices and be honest about the times I made the wrong ones. I could listen. I could bite my tongue when I was tempted to rant or preach. I could lean into my husband and other wise parents that could help me not climb up the crazy ledge once again. I could love my son even when I didn't like him or the choices he was making. I could cry out to God and tell him what I was afraid of and then leave my fears with him.

An important principle of lead measures is the word *predictive*. Doing these things doesn't guarantee anything. You can do everything to the best of your ability and your child can still get into scary things. But you need to know that the investment in fear and worry is no investment at all. You can focus on doing your best and then remind yourself that your best is all you can do.

WHEN LIFE GETS HARD

But let's be real. Watching your kids navigate their way through life can be incredibly painful. Sometimes our kids face things that are even out of *their* control. As moms we want to shield them and manipulate the circumstances and somehow make their road easier. There have been moments when I wanted to shrink my kids back to diapers and Sesame Street lunch boxes, when the problems they faced made sense and didn't have lasting implications. As my kids moved from babies to toddlers to children to teens, I began to realize how paralyzing mom fear could be.

When Brittainy was in seventh grade we noticed she was becoming more quiet and withdrawn. Shy as a preschooler, she had blossomed into a confident middle schooler, active in school and sports, but now we noticed she was spending more time alone in her room and was turning down opportunities for sleepovers and parties. One evening she and I went to a movie and about five minutes after it started, Brittainy got up to go to the bathroom. Twenty minutes went by and Brittainy hadn't come back. When I went to look for her, I found her lying on the bench in the movie lobby surrounded by people. Her words struck fear in my heart. "Mom, I think I'm having a heart attack."

In the hospital emergency room, the doctor quickly informed me she wasn't having a heart attack but rather a *panic attack*. A panic attack? What was she panicky about? The doctor asked me some questions. Had Geoff or I ever had panic attacks? No. Had Brittainy suffered a brain injury or other traumatic event? No! Even the question struck fear in my heart.

Over the course of the next few years, Geoff and I became immersed in learning about panic attacks. We found out that a panic attack is a sudden, intense feeling of fear or apprehension that made you feel like you were dying. You couldn't control when the attacks would occur and you usually couldn't stop them once they started. They made you feel as if something horrible was about to happen and that you needed to escape. Many times it affected your breathing and your heart rate and made you feel desperate. Many times what brought them on was a complete mystery. Even the doctors said they didn't completely understand them.

I don't have words to express how painful it was to watch Brittainy experience these painful attacks that stretched over the next few years, sometimes multiple times a day. They affected her confidence and her resilience. They seemed to suck the joy right out of her. I had to swallow the urge to panic right along with her. What could we, should we, have done to prevent them? Were they my fault? Wherever they had come from, whatever was the cause, I just wanted them to *stop this instant*.

I wish I could say I handled Brittainy's panic attacks with ease. I wish I could say I didn't let my fear run away with me. Neither of these was the case. The doctor reassured us there was nothing medically wrong with Brittainy and the panic attacks were certainly not going to kill her. They talked about medications and coping strategies. But inside I just got mad. *God, I know you love Brittainy more than I do. You can do anything. So why aren't you taking the panic attacks away?*

Maybe as a mom you've felt this way. We pray for our kids, we trust them completely to God. Why in the world does he let them go through pain and be exposed to things that are so devastating? I don't have the complete answer to these whys, but I do know that God has a plan for you as a mom, and for each one of your children from the moment they are born. God began to do some serious work on my heart and I began to learn what total trust was. I knew I couldn't stop Brittainy's attacks. All I could do was be there, reassure her, and let her know we were trying to help her as best we could.

LET'S GET PRACTICAL

When circumstances spin out of control, what is your initial reaction? Instead of panicking, try keeping a journal of resources in regard to a frightening situation. Keep track of references online and in books and make note of discussions with experts (in my case, doctors and counselors).

Surround yourself with people dealing with similar issues.

Support groups exist for many issues you or someone you love might be facing, and if there isn't a group meeting near you, find a support network online.

Pray, and ask those you love to pray, for a situation you are struggling with. You can't fix everything, but you can turn it over to a God whose shoulders can handle the burden.

GOD, MAKE MY KIDS DANGEROUS

One day as I was praying for Brittainy, I felt a question rise up in my heart. *What will Brittainy become?* In my heart I wasn't even letting my thoughts go there. I just wanted her to get past what she was dealing with today. Up to that time, I had always prayed, *God, keep my kids safe. Keep them from harm, protect them wherever they go.* As I began to spend some time dreaming hand in hand with God about what they could become instead of what I was afraid of right now, my thoughts changed, along with my fears. My prayers became refocused and proactive: *God, make my kids dangerous for you. Make Satan tremble at the sound of their voice. Make them so powerful that they change their world, instead of the world changing them.*

Looking back, I know God was dealing with my fear and my worry and my hopes and dreams for my kids, all wrapped up in one simple question, *What will Brittainy become?* I began to slowly trade my fear and worry for a big dream.

Today Brittainy is a worship leader who stands in front of crowds large and small. I look at her now and I see a strong young lady, imperfect but courageous. She still struggles with occasional panic attacks, but they don't throw her off course. She still faces fears and still has her moments of doubt, but I see her depending on a big God with a big plan.

So how about you? As a mom of little people or perhaps people on the road to adulthood, are you ready to make a trade? God is so ready to take your fear and replace it with a dream bigger than you've even imagined for your kids.

LET'S GET PRACTICAL

1. What scares you most about having teenagers? Are these fears based on things you have experienced or stories you have heard?
2. Do you have specific "crazy mama" fears that you struggle with? What are they? Do you have a husband or wise parent friends you can share them with?
3. What's the best "come down off the crazy ledge" advice that anyone has ever given you about being a mom?
4. What do you think God might be trying to say to you through this chapter?

LET'S TAKE ACTION

Put into words the dreams you have for your children. Start a Family Dream Journal and list out the dreams you feel God is giving you for your family. Consider sharing it with your husband and your children.

FACING YOUR
EMOTIONAL
MONSTERS

Up until now we have mainly been tackling hypothetical fears—fears of what could be. In this chapter we will begin to include real fears—fears of what *is*. The daunting fears, the truly emotional monsters brought on by the toughest things in life, like loss of employment, serious illness, accidents, divorce, and death. What do we do when the fear is no longer hypothetical or somewhere in the distant future but all too real and staring us in the face?

MOPS moms told us they fear their child being seriously hurt or injured. Running close behind this fear for many moms is a deep-seated anxiety about their own mortality: *What if something happens to me and I can't take care of my child?* Both of these fears are devastating to think about and some moms find it difficult to manage the emotions behind these fears.

For some of us, these thoughts are random occurrences related to our travels or time away from our children, but for others it's facing a real-life scary health situation that we can't brush away. It's these moments when we are afraid for ourselves and our kids that our emotions can really get the best of us. We feel trapped, unable to have hope for the future ahead. Janis, mom of three, shared an intimate story of facing the words no mom wants to hear. For her, it became a lesson in coming face-to-face with her fear, embracing truth, and learning to trust.

Pathway to Trust: Janis's Story

The words were spoken by the radiologist as he pointed to spots on the ultrasound film: "Ninety-five percent of the time this is cancer." The harsh words still echo in my mind sixteen years later. I wasn't usually one to beat the odds, so I knew I had just been diagnosed with breast cancer. One of my greatest fears was realized. I felt paralyzed and panicked, the emotion threatening to overwhelm me.

The next two weeks were some of the hardest days of my life, mainly because I didn't know what I was facing. What stage cancer did I have? What treatment was I going to face? How would this impact my family? Would I die from this? And if so, what would happen to my family, to my children? I went down an impossibly long, winding path of the unknown as one question after another swirled through my mind. In just a few days' time, my emotions ran the extremes of anger, denial, despair, and back again.

Gradually answers began to surface. My cancer was stage three and would require chemotherapy, radiation, and a lumpectomy. This type of cancer was very treatable with a high cure rate, but there weren't any guarantees. My family was supportive and caring, but it broke my heart to see them have to go through this. I came face-to-face with the fact that I had no choice but to trust God to care for my family if I couldn't. Once I knew the reality of the situation and what I was going to have to face, I felt more in control, and some of the fear was dissipated by a plan of action. There still wasn't a guaranteed outcome, but at least I was doing what I could to move forward.

So much of our fear is spent worrying about the unknown. Once we know the reality of a situation, we can usually face the consequences and begin to move forward. What I've come to realize from this experience and several overwhelmingly fearful experiences since then is that the stepping stone from fear to trust is often speaking and claiming truth.

Truth can be physical facts and information relevant to the fearful situation. To help me with my fear, I learned as much as I could by studying the research and understanding the statistics and data about my kind of cancer. Rationally, I knew that my kind of breast cancer was the "best" kind to have in terms of cure rates. I knew that many women had survived and even thrived in the midst of treatment and that there were systems in place to help me receive the best possible care. When my emotions would start to carry me away into hysterical fear, I clung to these physical truths to move me from fear to rational thinking.

More important than relying on physical truth was

clinging to spiritual truth. I claimed and personalized verses from Isaiah 43, *but this is what the Lord says— he who created you, Janis, he who formed you, Janis. Fear not, for I have redeemed you. I have summoned you by name. You are mine. When you pass through the waters, I will be with you.* I claimed this verse for my initial diagnosis and the dizzying decisions about which doctors and treatments to choose. There were moments when I felt as if I was drowning in the decisions, but I knew God had called me. I belonged to him.

I will be with you. And when you pass through the rivers, they will not sweep over you. When you walk through the fire, you will not be burned. The flames will not set you ablaze. I recited these words over and over as I looked ahead to the surgery and treatments that I would face. No matter what the outcome, I knew God was reassuring me he was in control.

Since you are precious and honored in my sight, and because I love you ... Do not be afraid for I am with you. I took these words to heart. God did love me, he was with me. I began to believe I could trade my fear for truth.

I also clung to the spiritual truth that God loved my children more than I did. My daughters were three and thirteen at the time of my diagnosis. After waiting ten years for our second daughter, I couldn't help but ask the question, would I now be taken out of her life? What about my oldest daughter who was thirteen? She was in such a vulnerable stage of life and at a tender place in her faith journey. Could I really trust God to be bigger than every scary part of this? These were the questions I wrestled with.

Clinging to Romans 8:38, I knew that nothing— neither death nor life, neither angels nor demons, neither the present nor the future, nor any powers, neither height nor depth, nor anything else in all creation (like cancer) could separate me (and those most precious to me) from the love of God that is in Christ Jesus. I wrote this verse down, and whenever fear would creep in, I would read it out loud to remind myself that God was faithful and could be trusted in the midst of my fear. As I claimed the truth of these verses, God replaced my fear with trust.

I've come to know that trust is the antidote to fear. When we trust God completely with our life and the lives of those most precious to us, we admit we are powerless to control the outcome, and we hand it over to the God who *is* in control. On a human level, it doesn't make sense, but I know God's love is all I need, and I trust in it. First John 4:18b says, "Perfect love drives out fear." This isn't talking about our need to love perfectly or to be perfect in our faith, in order to not be afraid. But rather, it's a call to experience

God's perfect love for us, the kind that covers us even when we crumble under the scary things before us. And when we do, our fear is replaced with complete trust in a faithful God.

Every time I climb on to a plane, I hand over the control of my life to the pilot. I trust he knows what he is doing. I've learned I can trust God even more. �֎

Moving Toward Solutions

Facing cancer is just one of many real-life situations where fear can grab hold of our emotions and take them for a scary ride. We know there are frightening things out there. We know we will face things bigger than ourselves. We know if we are not careful, our emotional monsters will take over, and then we are really in trouble. So what can we do about it? Let's talk about some general truths about fear and then move to some specific ways to attack it.

1. Fear will come knocking and will want to come in.

I love people, but I don't love salespeople who try to sell me something from my front door. When we first moved into our house in Denver, I was visited several times by a friendly but persistent salesman who desperately wanted to sell me fertilizer for my lawn. He knocked on my door and pointed out that my grass wasn't very happy and it was expressing it through its "lack of luster." I tried to show the proper amount of respect to this observation and engaged in a very boring discussion about Colorado grass types and its resistance to drought and cold temperatures.

Well, the salesman interpreted my passive response as a big *yes!* that we couldn't possibly live without his fertilizer, and proceeded to knock on my door five more times over the next week. I had to acknowledge my part in this. I had never come right out and been direct. *Thank you for your offer. We are not interested in fertilizer.* I did not have to get drawn into long discussions about grass, nor did I have to buy his fertilizer. What I did have to do though was be direct, acknowledge his offer, and say *no thanks.*

Sometimes we treat fear in the same way. We pretend around it and swat it away like an annoying fly, but until we deal with it directly, it's just going to come back. The best way to keep your emotions under control is to acknowledge what's scary, deal with it, and move on.

2. While fear is very real, it doesn't have to paralyze you.

This one gets me every time. Just because a scary thought hits me, it doesn't mean I have to ruminate on it, letting my emotions get carried away with every possible scenario. Just as Janis shared in her story, she could have chosen to dwell on how serious her situation was, but instead she focused on the factual information about her cancer and her course of action. Our emotions can get so big in the midst of fear that we literally freeze, unable to stop worrying long enough to do anything about it. As we'll discuss in this chapter, this doesn't have to be.

Some moms worry they won't have what it takes to handle

a serious emergency, like an accident involving blood or broken bones. No one can plan for every possible emergency, but let me assure you that your mom instincts will kick in, and you will move quickly to do whatever you can to address the situation, whether that's calling 911 or grabbing a towel to stop the flow of blood. In the midst of an accident involving your child, God will give you the strength to respond to the best of your ability and adrenaline will help you act past your fears.

3. The goal is not to eliminate fear, but to manage it.

Wouldn't it be great if we could wave our arms and voilà, we aren't scared of anything ever again? We all know this isn't reasonable. Trying to avoid every scary situation as a mom isn't in the realm of possibility, nor is it healthy to try. But it is possible to be the best brave mom you can be, who has go-to strategies that come naturally to you when you face tough situations. Become a student of yourself. How have you handled fear or scary situations in the past? Can you identify the times you handled fear well? By reminding yourself of your own resilience and ability to cope, you can begin to prepare yourself for future challenges.

WHAT'S IN A NAME?

In dealing with my fear of flying, it helped to give what scared me most a name: turbulence. With that one word, the windy, bumpy mess that knocked the plane around was downsized to a single word. To even say it out loud made it seem much more manageable. I think we can apply the same principle to our fears. What exactly are we dealing with? Once we know, we can start to aim some strategies directly at it.

Are you dealing with panic?

Panic is characterized by sudden uncontrollable fear and anxiety and usually accompanied by a fierce desire to *get away*, *get out*, *do something right now*. The good news about dealing with panic is that you can train yourself to stop, take a deep breath, and talk yourself down off the ledge. One way I consistently do this is to have short, go-to Bible verses that speak comfort to my head and heart. I repeat them to myself, sometimes just one phrase over and over.

> The LORD is my light and my salvation — whom shall I fear? (Psalm 27:1a)

> God has said, "'Never will I leave you; never will I forsake you.' So we say with confidence, 'The Lord is my helper; I will not be afraid. What can mere mortals do to me?'" (Hebrews 13:5b, – 6)

> When I am afraid, I put my trust in you. (Psalm 56:3)

When you recognize that you are in the midst of a panic, admit it and state what you will do. *I'm feeling panicky and I'm going to change the way I feel by filling my head with God's truth.*

Please do note, however, that panicky feelings are not the

same as a full-blown panic attack. If you think you may be having panic attacks, consult with your doctor. As I discovered with my daughter, medication and help are available for this very common illness. And if you are not sure whether your anxiety is passing or more serious — don't wait and wonder. Bring the concern to your doctor's attention.

Are you dealing with irrational thoughts?

Irrational thoughts can sneak up on you, and having them doesn't make you crazy, but they can take you for a crazy ride. We've already shown how irrational thoughts can crop up in hypothetical situations (*that sound was someone trying to break in and we are all going to die!*), but they can be even worse when you are facing a true crisis (*my son was diagnosed with autism — will he be dependent on me the rest of his life?*).

When you find yourself getting ready to board the crazy train of irrational thinking, stop yourself with a question. *Is this likely to happen?* There is a big difference between possible and probable. *Probable* means it is likely, that the odds are in favor of it happening. We do need to take precautions and be sensible, but we make ourselves miserable by worrying about things that are possible, which most of the time means unlikely.

Ask yourself some secondary questions: *Does this usually happen under these circumstances? Am I worrying about something that is unlikely?* Remind yourself of the likely outcome. *That noise is just the house shifting. There are many therapies, schools, and organizations that can help me raise my child and address his autism.*

If a situation is so serious that difficult consequences are *probable,* you will need to return to the truth and comfort that God is in control. When you find yourself in the midst of frightening circumstances that you can *respond* to, but cannot alter — this is the time to lean into a God who knows your deepest fears and can carry you through anything. "Trust in the LORD with all your heart and lean not on your own understanding." (Proverbs 3:5)

When you find yourself in the midst of irrational thinking, admit it and state what you will do. *I'm getting carried away with irrational thoughts that are very unlikely and I am going to redirect my thinking by focusing on the facts and stating the probable.*

Are you dealing with denial?

Pretending we are not afraid means we haven't dealt with it. Just like that pesky salesman, the fear will continue to come back until we firmly let it know we mean business. Hopefully in this book you've had a few "me too" moments when you've realized other moms deal with the same fears that you do. We all deal with fear and it's okay to admit it. If you have recurring fears, panic, or irrational thoughts — consider naming them out loud. Putting words to your feelings and saying them to someone else boils them down to size and takes their power away.

If the situation you are facing is serious, denying your fear also means denying yourself, and maybe even your children, the help and the support that you desperately need. Turning a blind eye to your son's drinking won't help him. Sweeping marital strife under the rug is not a solution. Any ongoing issue you are fearful about is only compounded by ignoring it. It can be just as bad to minimize a fear as it is to maximize one, so being "fearless" does not necessarily put you off the hook for dealing with fear (isn't that ironic?).

If you have thought being a Christ follower means you never deal with fear and you are ashamed of it, get rid of that thought right now. God doesn't condemn us for our fear; he offers to help us with it. And if you are using your faith to avoid dealing with a serious situation (*God will heal him so rehab won't be necessary*), remember that God may be more interested in making you or your child grow spiritually through a struggle than in miraculously and instantly "fixing" the situation to your liking.

If you think you might be in denial or minimizing your fear, find a trusted friend to admit it to, and check up on yourself. *I'm not as brave as you might think. I find myself pretending away my fears, so if I ever do that, I want you to let me know. I'm trusting you won't judge me or think I'm crazy, but that you'll help me deal with my denial. If you see something serious in my life that I should do something about, I want you to help me face it. In fact, right now there's an issue that I might not be taking as seriously as I should. Can you help me think it through?*

Do your fears bring depression?

This can be a never-ending cycle. When fear attacks us, it can make us feel powerless and depressed. When we are depressed, we feel hopeless, which can make us fearful. It's normal to feel blue, but if you feel overwhelmed by fear and depression and unable to break out of this pattern of thinking, it might be time to consider talking to a professional. I have found Christian counselors to be extremely helpful. They have helped me to find the rational path and to understand my thinking patterns. They have encouraged me toward healthy, productive solutions.

It's powerful to surround yourself with others who can bring perspective to your thinking, whether it's a professional or a group of friends. The pesky thing about depression and fear is that it makes us want to hide, to be alone. This is the opposite of what is really helpful. If you find yourself dealing with depressed thoughts that perpetuate your fear, acknowledge them and state what you will do. *I feel depressed and fearful, so I will break this cycle by partnering with a trusted professional, mentor, or circle of mom friends that I can talk to.*

Depression isn't a myth — it is a real illness that affects millions of people, and it doesn't make you weak or "less than" to admit that you are suffering from depression. *It makes you brave.* Fear can absolutely manifest itself physically in the form of depression and panic attacks, and there is also a physiological component to these afflictions. Hormones and brain chemistry both affect our state of well-being and the mental and emotional turmoil, physical exhaustion, mental fog, and other symptoms that are part of depression can be helped by a variety of medications, counseling, and other forms of therapy. Don't be ashamed, and do seek help.

LET'S ATTACK!

As wise moms will tell you, the best defense is a prepared offense. We slather tender bottoms with the best diaper rash medicine. We whip out the thermometer faster than you can utter the word *fever*. We make sure our kids are layered and buttoned and booted at the first hint of cold weather. Why in the world wouldn't we arm ourselves with tried and true fear busters? As many moms shared their stories of what they feared most, they also shared some of their go-to strategies to deal with their fears and worries before they got out of control.

Do a laundry sort.

Just like we sort the colors from the whites, Colleen, mom of five, says she sorts her fears into two piles: things I have control over and things I don't. She said the way she determines this is by asking herself, *Is there anything I can do about it?* She said if it is a situation over which she has no control, such as her son is out with the car, she puts it in the prayer-and-trust pile. She tells God what she is nervous about, acknowledges that she doesn't have control, and asks God to give her heart peace. Then she gets her mind busy on other things.

If it is a fear she can do something about, such as check to make sure the doors are locked or that the power tool is unplugged and out of reach of her five-year-old, she takes action. Then she tells herself out loud, *Okay, I've done all I can do!* She says she gets bossy with her thoughts and forces herself to not drive herself crazy with the *what ifs*.

Pick your friends wisely.

My friend Betsy shared a story about a friend she had that took her thoughts to places she didn't want to go. Every time she shared a fear or worry with this friend, she walked away worried about more things than were originally on her mind. Instead of helping her with reasonableness, the friend caused her to worry even more by piling on fears of her own. Betsy found she had to limit her time with this friend.

If you have people in your life who add fuel to your fears, you may need to follow Betsy's lead and instead lean on those I call the unshakeables. These are the folks who don't panic, but seem to face situations with a steady calm. Look around for someone who seems to radiate a sense of calm wisdom. These are the people I try to spend time with, especially when I feel fear and worry calling my name.

My friend Sibyl is such a friend. She always has a positive outlook and helps me to examine the worst possible outcome of my fears, making me realize that even if the worst came true, it wasn't as bad as I was imagining. Do your friends fuel your fear or give you confidence to battle through it? This is a great gauge to use when choosing who you will spend time with.

Get some accountability and support.

I'm a big believer in letting others help and I have found tremendous gain in a mentor who holds me accountable in the areas I want to grow. Early in my life as a mom, I set a goal to be the best mom my kids could ever need or want. It sounds lofty, doesn't it? While I certainly didn't aim for perfection, I did want to be the best I could be, but I knew I would need help. I looked for an older mom whose wisdom I trusted, and we started to meet regularly. She listened to the areas I wanted to grow in and held me accountable by asking me the same three questions every time:

How are you doing?

How are you doing with your kids?

How are you and God doing?

She asked me these questions because she already knew what I didn't. It wasn't just about keeping the house organized or packing the best lunches, it was about how I was doing on the inside, managing my emotional self and my resilient core. She also knew that it was more about the relationship between me and my kids versus what I was doing for my kids. She also knew these things had to be anchored in a firm relationship with God. I knew these questions were coming every time we met, so I made sure I paid attention to them between times.

Sara, a mom of two, says she has an accountability mentor to help her grow through her fear. Her mentor asks her these questions every time:

Are you writing in your Courage Journal regularly?

Are you focusing on what's true instead of what you are afraid of?

Are you reminding yourself of your life verse when you feel panicky? (Her life verse is Jeremiah 29:11.)

Knowing that someone is going to regularly ask you how you are handling your fear is an incredible tool to help you grow through it.

Frisk your thoughts at the door.

Where does fear come from? We've discussed in this book that fear can enter our thoughts based on what we've seen and heard. We are faced every day with stories of disasters, accidents, and children gone missing. The newspapers, Internet, and media feed our fear. But here's what I've learned: I can't control every scary thing, but I can control whether or not these things strike fear in my heart. And the fear of these things doesn't come from God. Second Timothy 1:7 says, "For God gave us not a spirit of fearfulness, but of power and love and discipline" (ASV). Just as I don't let every stranger into my house, I don't have to let every thought come into my mind.

Author and Bible teacher Kay Arthur suggests that we can "frisk our thoughts" by passing them through the grid of Philippians 4:8. Are they true, honorable, just, pure, lovely, commendable, morally excellent, and praiseworthy? This doesn't describe fear. Fear is dark, scary, and isolating. When fear comes, you can pat it down at the door of your mind, just like a TSA agent. If it doesn't match up to Philippians 4:8, don't invite it in.

Jana, mom of Grace, says having her first child filled her with fear she didn't know she had. What if Grace got hurt? What if she fell asleep and didn't hear Grace crying? What if Grace got sick and she didn't know what to do? She said at times the fear was overwhelming. It wasn't until her mom told her that this is exactly the way Satan wanted her to feel, that she began to question where these thoughts were coming from. Was this a good, encouraging thought? Or was it a dark, threatening one? She said she started asking God, *Is this from you? Should I even be thinking about this?* She said she has become an expert at catching imposter thoughts at the door and shutting them down!

Choose gratitude.

Fear makes us feel small and hopeless. What makes us feel the opposite? For Gina, mom of three, it is when she has a thankful heart. Gina says she forces herself to think about all the good in her life because it opens her heart and lifts her eyes to bigger things. Gina says, "It's hard to be scared when you are thinking about things that bring you joy."

There have been times when I have had a hard time focusing my mind on the joyful parts of my life instead of the discouraging, fearful parts. Those are the moments I start "thankful" lists. I literally begin to make a list of all the things I'm thankful for, starting with my family and then moving to all the things and opportunities God has given me. I challenge myself to keep going when I think I've written everything I can think of. It's amazing how this simple exercise can change the course of your thinking.

Get busy.

It's true. Sometimes the simplest form of changing your thoughts is to distract them. I have found the Scarlett O'Hara method of avoidance has its wisdom with the line, "I won't think of it now. I'll think of it later when I can stand it." Sometimes getting bossy with yourself and then getting busy is the best course of action. It's hard to control your thoughts, so sometimes buying yourself some time to return to rational thinking by doing something else with your hands is a good strategy.

Joan, mom of two, says that fear hits her when she's home alone and has time to worry. She hates to clean so if she finds herself caught up in needless fear and worry, she "fines" herself by making herself clean the house. She says pretty soon she's distracted herself enough to forget what was overtaking her thoughts. Plus she ends up with a clean house as a bonus!

It's a wise mom that admits she has fear, knows what the emotions are that she's dealing with, and then designs strategies to attack them. Let's pause and take some time to make sure you've fully stocked your strategy tool belt.

LET'S GET PRACTICAL

1. Have you dealt with a serious situation like Janis's illness that filled you with emotional fear? How did you handle your fear?
2. Can you identify the type of fear you are dealing with? Do you struggle with panic, irrational thoughts,

denial, or depression, or do you struggle with something else?

3. Did any of the fear strategies mentioned above resonate with you? Are there any others that you employ when fear hits?

LET'S TAKE ACTION

Have you ever started a thankfulness list? Consider keeping a running list of people, experiences, and things that you are truly thankful for. Challenge yourself to constantly be thinking of things to add to your list. Share it with your husband, support partner, or mentor, and note how it changes your thinking toward fear.

8

BUILDING
A BETTER YOU

s it possible to be a mom and not lose it? When your children are fully grown into normal, functional adults, is it possible to still be in possession of your faculties, meaning you haven't lost your ever-loving mind? I pondered this one morning as Mike and Brittainy sat at the kitchen table hurling insults at each other. They had stacked the cereal boxes between them on the table so that they did not have to endure even the sight of each other's face. Mike kicked his sister under the table. Brittainy responded with a slap at his head that caused the cereal box fortress to crumble, knocking his bowl full of milk to the floor. For crying out loud, I just wanted to move far, far away, somewhere like Australia.

They are adorable when they appear on the scene, aren't they? They join the world with precious little fists curled up next to their tiny little faces, uttering soft little coos that melt our heart. They smell so sweet. We watch them sleeping so innocently in their cribs and dream of what they will become. Then they grow up with mouths that utter sass that brings the gray to our hair. They smell like wind and wild sweat. They step in dog poop and track it on our carpet. They make messes, they make mistakes, and they make us worry. We begin to realize that we can no longer protect them from everything the world might offer them or fling their way. We realize with a sense of finality that we can't control their world.

Throughout your life as a mom, you will be nose wiper, bottom inspector, referee, comforter, counselor, and the grand giver of hugs. You will serve not only as mom, but you will fulfill the duties of protector, guardian, chief detective, and whistle blower. Your heart will be thrilled and stretched, pulled and challenged. Add the possibilities of dangerous opportunities, scary situations, and possible injuries, and it's a wonder every mom doesn't run from the room screaming at the first glimpse of the positive response on the pregnancy test.

Yet with all the challenges full of fear and worry, there are moms who not only survive, but thrive. They face the same obstacles and opportunities to panic, but they hold steady. What makes the difference? Are there secrets these moms know that others don't? Are there habits or practices that help them overcome the challenges of fear and worry, tantrums and sass?

Several years ago, MOPS International began a research study to ask these exact questions. What separates the moms who flourish and thrive in parenting from the ones who don't? What gives a mom the confidence and support she needs to be the best mom possible? How can a mom become so resilient that she won't crumble under the weight of her fear or anxiety? By targeting our questions specifically at *what makes a better mom* and *how does she make a better world*, we discovered five attributes that moms self-identified that contribute to a better mom. These attributes make her stronger, more resilient, and more effective.

WHAT MAKES A BETTER MOM?

What do we mean by a "better mom"? MOPS invested significant time to conduct preliminary research in the form of focus groups with various constituents, primarily moms of young children and the leaders who lead them, to identify common denominators and characteristics that could help define a "better" mom. In addition, extensive secondary research was conducted to review government and secular studies that examined successful parenting practices. We also partnered with the Barna Group to develop specific questions that identified how confident a mom felt within each of these common denominators and what it meant to her success as a healthy, well-balanced mom. As a result of this research, MOPS came up with five contributing factors that comprised *The Better Mom, Better World Metric*, defining what makes a "better mom." We'll state them simply here then spend some time unpacking their implications later in the chapter.

1. A better mom develops a significant support system.

We found that moms who not only had friends, but a network of trusted support to run to when parenting became overwhelming, fared much better. The support system could include parents, extended family, older moms, babysitters, counselors, teachers, or mom friends in the same life stage, but were all people she felt she could turn to for childcare, answers, or just a supporting hug that said *you're going to be okay.* For these moms, being surrounded by such a network on a regular, continuing basis was probably the single most important key to becoming a better mom. For stay-at-home moms especially, motherhood can be a 24/7 job, and frankly *no one* is equipped to work 24/7. Having childcare help on call in the form of a babysitter, daycare, or family member becomes crucial. And it's important to take advantage of these resources by taking a few hours off, or even a day off, from the kids from time to time to relax and renew.

Not only do moms need practical support, they do better with emotional support as well, which is why mom groups that meet regularly throughout the year and are comprised of moms in similar stages — such as MOPS groups — are of particular importance. And no, we didn't "stack the deck" to make sure we got this result! Of course, MOPS began over 40 years ago with the idea that moms do better with social support, but we are delighted to find that the latest research still supports the importance of our mission. Some moms find this support through play groups, book groups, exercise classes, school volunteer work, Bible studies, church small groups, or work colleagues, but no matter where, the better mom has typically found a group to support herself in one or more areas of her life.

2. A better mom works to develop her parenting knowledge and skills.

We've already established that there is no perfect mom or perfect child, and within that we know there are no one-size-fits-all rules for parenting. But the mom who thrives consistently surrounds herself with opportunities to develop the knowledge and skill to parent well. She reads parenting books, blogs, magazines, and websites. She asks friends, family, and mentors parenting questions. She observes what works and doesn't work in the parenting styles she sees around her. She learns about child development stages, finds discipline techniques that work for her and her child, and develops practices to deal with the everyday challenges, whether that is breastfeeding an infant, potty training a toddler, or helping a child who is struggling in school. No matter her child's age or stage, she never "coasts" but is constantly on the lookout for ways to improve herself as a mother. In fact, both my children are out of the nest, and I'm still learning how to parent them in an entirely new season for all of us!

3. A better mom has a healthy marriage or significant parenting partner.

A better mom often has a healthy, growing marriage that provides her with someone to support her on a daily basis. But we know that an increasing number of children are being raised in single-parent homes. According to statistics in *The Atlantic*, single moms account for precisely one quarter of US households.[17] Single moms were also part of our study, and we found that those who thrived made concerted efforts to connect with someone who could help them in a significant way, such as the child's father, their mother, or a sister. In some ways this is just a restatement of #1 — that better moms have a significant support system — but it acknowledges the key, serious, and ongoing support that can best be supplied by marriage or family.

4. Better moms have developed core resilience.

Core resilience refers to the emotional components that play a significant part in a mom's well-being. A strong, resilient mom pays attention to her emotional needs, listens to what is going on in her mind and body, and doesn't hesitate to ask for help. A meaningful part of this attribute is having the self-awareness to know what you need when you need it. A healthy core resilience allows you to be optimistic under pressure, to deal with stress effectively, to maintain your sense of humor, and to bounce back after facing significant setbacks or challenges. Core resilience isn't innate, and it is not the same thing as self-confidence — this state-of-being is developed through practical applications like prayer, sometimes counseling, and honest relationships with friends.

5. A better mom pays attention to her spiritual development.

We asked moms how significantly their relationship with God impacted their role as mom. Moms who rated themselves as stronger and more confident identified that they had a strong connection with a local church, and an ongoing relationship with God that they identified as a source of strength and help. Moms like this realized that spiritual growth required more than attending Sunday services, and among other things demanded personal, daily spiritual habits of prayer and Bible reading.

The Seven Habits of Better Moms

Within the five attributes we began to gather practical habits that moms shared with us that helped them face the daily challenges and fears with confidence in a healthy, resilient way. We know that every mom will face frustrations and fears and will question at times whether she is a good enough mom, but what are the habits of those who feel they are prepared to handle these challenges in a better way when they come? Through anecdotal research, we've gathered seven practical habits that help a mom develop the strength and confidence she needs to truly become a better mom.

1. Better moms form a SWAT team of support.

SWAT is a military acronym that stands for Special Weapons And Tactics. It refers to the arsenal and process by which soldiers are prepared for any upcoming attacks and includes a variety of support and options. We have found that healthy, resilient moms think the same way in that they don't rely on just one source of support. They surround themselves with mentors and supportive friends, participate in mom growth and support groups, and take advantage of the resources that are presented or discussed, such as parenting books or classes. The point is they know they can't rely on just their own wisdom and that being a mom can be isolating and lonely, so they always have a source to go to for help.

I recently talked with a young mom named Beth, who said she has two different mentors that she meets with occasionally, one who is older and has grown children, and another who has children the same age, from within her MOPS group. She goes to them for different purposes. She talks with the older mom when she's not sure if her fears are reasonable, asking questions such as, *Did your children ever face this? Should I be worried about this?* The older mom prays with her, which she says is a tremendous comfort. With the younger mom she compares experiences and asks more age-related questions: *How are you getting your child to sleep alone in his bed? What are you doing to encourage your child to make friends?* Beth knows that using different mentors in different situations helps her more than limiting herself to just one.

One day my phone rang and I was immediately intrigued because the mom on the other end was using her whisper voice.

"Sherry, it's Amy. What are you up to?"

"Amy? What are *you* up to? Why are you whispering?"

She hesitated. "I'm in the garage. I'm hiding from the kids."

Amy was a young mom of three boys, two of them two-year-old twins, and she began to share the story that landed her in the garage. She had put her twins in a timeout in their room after their very hectic morning of coloring on the wall, smearing jelly on the coffee table, and giving the cat a successful makeover with her lipstick. She had endured all she could take, so she walked them calmly to the room they shared and told them to lie down on their beds. It wasn't long before she heard a banging noise. When she entered their room, she saw they had stacked their toy chests on top of each other and were using their plastic Bob the

Builder toy tools to try to take the door off its hinges. She said the sad thing was they were making progress!

She was calling me from the garage, where she had retreated with a bag of Oreos because she had to call someone who wouldn't call her crazy for hiding. I told her I understood and shared the story of how two-year-old Mike had gotten a hankering for scrambled eggs and had cracked half a dozen on the kitchen floor before I caught him.

I assured Amy that hiding in the garage eating her secret stash of chocolate didn't make her crazy. The fact that she reached out to talk about it with another mom friend who would understand made her a very wise mama indeed.

2. Better moms prioritize their spiritual development and find a spiritual rhythm that works for them.

Moms are notorious for making sure everyone in the family has what they need. Does everyone have their lunch? Check. Does everyone have their backpack and the notes for the teacher signed and ready? Check. But who is making sure that mom has everything *she* needs? Healthy moms will sometimes let themselves slide to last on the list when it comes to meals or supplies, but they prioritize when it comes to their spiritual development. They know that a few minutes of quiet time journaling, praying, or reading their Bible feeds their soul and helps them stand fast in the times of crisis, so they don't let themselves scrimp in this area. Morgan, mom of two, said this, "I don't have an hour to invest in Bible study every day, but I do get up a few minutes before everyone else when the house is nice and quiet. I need the extra sleep, but I know I need that time to hear from God even more."

Moms who found themselves pressed for time often would schedule "quiet time" on their calendar like an appointment, to get their attention. One mom noted that the things she scheduled got done. She admitted there were always other pressing things that needed her attention, but she has decided to prioritize. "I never miss a doctor's appointment because it is officially on my calendar. I do the same for my God time."

Not only do better moms focus on developing themselves spiritually, they also find a spiritual rhythm that works with their personality or current stage of life. Julianna, mom of three, admits that she doesn't like to journal, but she does write down her prayers. She says this helps keep her weary brain focused and she finds writing things down causes her to slow down enough to really think about what she wants to say to God. She says sometimes when she is really worried about something, she will write it down and then close the book with a snap, as if to say, *I'm done worrying about that. Now it belongs to you, God!*

Healthy, resilient moms don't waste time on spiritual practices that don't fit their personality or life. Instead they invest in the ones that do. Busy moms will often tell me they talk to God while walking with the baby outside, or while jogging in the morning, or while finishing up the dishes late at night when the house is quiet. Lindsey, mom of five, said her laundry is never finished, and while she sits and folds the clothes, she prays. The point is that these healthy moms find a way to connect with God that is doable and meaningful to them. They don't try to copy what someone else does. They find their own rhythm.

3. Better moms invest in who they were before they were a mom.

On my way home from work every day, I pass a park with a fun climbing structure and several sets of swings. Driving by I would remember my favorite childhood park and how I would swing for hours, enjoying the feel of the wind in my hair. One day, as I was thinking about the material for this book, I realized I hadn't been on a swing in many years. Why not? I love to swing. Who says mamas with grown children and saggy arms can't swing? I pulled the car over and walked straight to an empty swing.

I learned two things. First, my behind is much larger than it was when I was a girl. I learned those swings are made for skinny little seven-year-old bottoms and mine is not. The second thing I learned was that I still loved to swing. The wind in my hair was just as exhilarating as it had been years ago. Swinging still lifted my spirits and made me laugh out loud. Swinging was fun!

Why is it that when we become a mom, we often abandon the things that we loved before? We still go to the park, but we are often the pusher of the swing instead of the rider. We become the responsible ones. We take over the thinking and planning and worrying. We lose our joy.

We learned from healthy moms that they cultivate their joy by staying in touch with the things they loved before they had kids. Karen, mom of one, said she still makes tennis dates with her friends, partly to stay in shape but also because she just flat-out loves the game. She says after a Saturday morning of tennis she comes back more relaxed and in a better frame of mind to handle all that is going on in their household. Stephanie, a brand new mom, says she is almost overcome every day with worrying about their daughter Carrie Ann, who was born with heart problems. As a little girl herself, she used to spend hours on what she called her "nothing books." They were bundles of paper folded over into a booklet, and she would spend Sunday afternoons filling them with pictures she cut from magazines and the newspaper. She said there was no rhyme or reason to the books, but just the making of them made her happy. She said she recently took up this hobby again because the mindless acts of cutting and pasting helped her relax.

How wise these moms are to invest in things they know bring them happiness and help them relax. One of the best gifts we can give our children is to show them what we enjoy doing and let them see us continuing to invest in our joy.

4. Better moms allow themselves the margin they need.

My friend Janni is a wise and healthy mom of two girls. After her second child was born, she found a way to take what she called a "Mental Health Day." Janni and her husband didn't have extra money for babysitters, but she didn't let this stop her. She traded babysitting days with another young mom and took a half day off every week to just go "be a person." She said sometimes she would walk outside in another neighborhood away from her house or walk through the mall and window shop. Other days she would take a thermos of tea and just find a quiet place to sit and think. She knew she needed time away from her responsibilities as a wife and mom, and she gave herself permission to take it. She forced herself to think of other things besides her children. When she would catch herself in a worrying thought, she nipped it in the bud by telling herself, "For the next few minutes I'm thinking happy thoughts." She took time to breathe deep and notice the things around her. She forced herself to smile and took time to think about herself and what she needed.

This is what healthy moms do. They listen to their bodies and their inner voices. They recognize when "mama is about to blow," and they take action. Do you find yourself needing some time away from the little people who won't even allow you to pee in peace? Give yourself permission to take a mini vacation. You'll find even short times away will help you recalibrate and be able to reclaim your resilient, healthy self.

5. Better moms keep their sense of humor.

By now almost everyone knows that laughter has incredible health benefits, including relaxing the body, reducing stress, and boosting the immune system.

Taking time to laugh is incredibly important, especially to

young moms who find themselves consumed with worry and fear. Your sense of humor can be a powerful tool in your arsenal for fighting fear. We all know taking time to laugh is important, but why do we find ourselves going days without it? I think sometimes we forget how funny life really can be.

My friend Lindsey, mom of four boys, shared this story. One day the doorbell rang and when she opened the door she found a police officer standing on their doorstep. The officer introduced himself and said he was there because he had gotten a call from a neighbor reporting she had seen naked people running around in their yard. Just then, their middle son walked up wearing nothing but his tennis shoes. She looked down and said, "Officer, I think we have found the problem." The officer looked at her, then looked at her son, smiled, and said, "Keep it up, boy!"

I'm sure Lindsey had a moment when she wondered what nosy neighbor had the time to watch out the window and call the police because her children were running around the yard in their birthday suits. I'm sure she had more than one moment of frustration with her children wondering why no one listened to her when she instructed the people in her house to keep their clothes on. I'm sure it didn't feel funny to greet a policeman at her door and have to explain all of the above. But she chose to laugh. Moms, laughter is good for us. It keeps our faces from looking drawn and tight and keeps that saggy, old lady neck at bay. It helps us feel young and keeps our heart light and speaks joy to our children. It keeps us sane. It makes us better moms.

6. Better moms invest in their marriage.

Here is what I know about my husband, Geoff. He wants to be my provider and wants to know he is doing a good job of taking care of my needs. He wants to be my knight in shining armor to swoop in with a solution when I need him. He wants to be my friend. But here is how I often treat him: I take him for granted. I ignore him until I really need something that I don't know how to tackle (or don't want to tackle), like the flat tire on my car or the backed-up garbage disposal (I refuse to stick my hand down there). I nag at him to do things on my time schedule and dump the remains of my bad day on him in the form of crabby complaints. Geoff and I have been married for thirty years and it has taken me years to realize investing in my marriage is really an investment in a healthier, happier me. We found that healthy moms know this and don't ignore even the smallest of opportunities to invest wisely here.

My friend Sharon, mom of three, says that one thing she and her husband like to do is play cards in bed. They are both competitive, and playing cards is something that draws them together at the end of the day. They keep a running game of Cribbage going and depending on how tired they are, they may only play a hand or two. They decided long ago that they would keep the fun in their marriage and their card-playing ritual has become one of their favorite times of their day.

Sally, mom of two young boys, loves to celebrate holidays and special times. As a family they celebrate the usual holidays and birthdays, but she reserves certain days that are special only to her and her husband. She reminds her husband of these days — such as their first date, the day she told him they were pregnant with their first child, and the day they bought their first house — but she takes care of any celebration plans. Why? Because, she says, they were a couple before the kids came and they will be a couple after they leave. This is a wise mama who knows that the investment in her marriage will pay off in huge dividends to her personally.

If you are a mom who is married, think now about small ways you can invest in your marriage by spending time having fun together. Don't make excuses when it comes to romance. Let him see the woman he fell in love with before your wonderful kids came. Your days are long and your body is exhausted, but your husband can be an incredible source to lean on and can be a rock of strength and help. Don't shut him out when it comes to sharing your fears, and listen when he offers a different perspective. I used to think I would be letting Geoff down if I shared how often I was overcome by fears and worries, and I sometimes wondered if he would think I was crazy. Instead I found he was willing to share his as well and it made me feel better just to say it out loud with someone who knew me so well.

If you are a mom who isn't married, don't waste a moment on regret or worry. Instead, find a support partner. Someone you can laugh with, someone who will listen to your fears and offer support. The important thing is to realize that being a mom is too big of a job to do alone.

7. Better moms parent with the end in mind.

Emotionally healthy, resilient moms don't panic. They realize that the tantrums of today are just that: symptoms of what is going on in the moment, not indications of what will always be. The messes and fits that are a daily occurrence don't throw them because they know they are just the building blocks to the adults they will become. Healthy moms remind themselves that rarely does a child start school not potty trained and that refusing to eat carrots won't scar them for life. They will mature, they will grow, and they will change their mind.

Erin, mom of middle school son Mark, said she chooses to take the "long view" when it comes to her son. His wild opinions that he has today probably won't be a part of him tomorrow. Why worry about them now or try to argue him out of them when she can just wait and see?

Healthy moms know they are not building the children of today, they are shaping the adults of tomorrow. And because they know what a world-changing job this is, they refuse to throw up their hands in defeat. They keep trying.

The great news about the Seven Habits of Better Moms is that these are habits we can all develop. In chapter two I mentioned that the second beautiful truth of being a mom is that great moms don't happen by accident. The corollary of this is they do happen on purpose. By focusing on just one habit, you can build your confidence as a mom and be better equipped to handle the fears and worries that come your way. Ready to begin? Let's get started!

LET'S GET PRACTICAL

1. Which of the Seven Habits would you most like to develop in your life? Why?
2. What are three things you will do on a regular basis to help you develop this habit? Brainstorm some ideas with a few mom friends to help you get started.
3. Who will hold you accountable for developing this habit? Write their name here.

LET'S TAKE ACTION

An action plan or goal is most effective when it is written with clear steps and has a time frame. Write out your three action steps and commit to a date by which you will complete them.

9

HELPING YOUR
CHILD BE BRAVE

It was a great day to be outside at the pool, especially on such a hot Houston day. Mike had been playing with friends in the shallow end but had stopped to watch the older kids, as they wrestled at the deep end, took daring steps back, and then hurled themselves over the edge with abandon. Their heads went down, down, into the water and they soon emerged, gasping and laughing. Mike watched their every move, the look in his eyes a mixture of awe and wonder.

After a while he came over to where I was sitting with another mom. "Mom, can I jump? I mean a real jump, without my floaties and you won't catch me?"

I hesitated as I looked at him standing before me, dripping wet with his Spider-Man swim trunks at half mast, barely covering his skinny four-year-old behind. My mom heart was so captivated by the eager look on his face. He so wanted to join in with the big guys. I agreed, but moved to the pool edge to watch. Just in case.

I could tell he had an inner battle going on as he walked toward the deep end. He knew he could jump, but he also knew his face would go completely under. We had taught him how to swim (okay, dog paddle) to the edge, but I could tell he was contemplating the distance. One minute it was a look of confidence, the next a moment of panic. I wondered, *Will he go for it? Should he go for it?*

My mom fear was engaged in an inner battle as well. I wanted

Mike to have fun, to be adventurous, but I didn't want him to get hurt. I wanted him to try new things and not let fear hold him back, but I didn't want him to be reckless. I felt a niggling fear ripple through my stomach. *Should I be letting him do this?* I knew I was letting my mom angst get me into a twist over a simple jump into the pool. And then — he jumped! He paddled to the edge! *And I smiled and breathed a sigh of relief.*

The next day was a trip to the park. Mike had been looking forward to going on what he called the "big slide," a climbing apparatus that boasted a tall yellow slide that looked slippery and steep. Mike chattered the whole way and when we got there, it was teeming with noisy, chattering children of all ages — girls screeching their laughter and boys daringly pushing each other off the slide steps. I could tell by the look on Mike's face that he wanted so badly to join in. He had been looking forward to this trip to the park, but now he just wanted to go home. It was too crowded, too loud, too much. He cowered back, chewing on his fingers, his eyes never leaving the crowded mass of kids.

I so wanted to help, but all I knew to do was give him gentle encouragements. He loved to wrestle with his cousins and could push and shove with the best of them, but lately I had noticed him back off from large groups of kids when the play got too loud or too rough for his liking. My mind wandered over the possibilities. *Was this too boisterous of an experience for a four-year-old, or was he experiencing ordinary shyness? Did the rough play actually scare him, even though this wasn't anything to be afraid of? This was normal for a preschooler, right?*

Then I caught myself. Yesterday I was worried that Mike was not scared enough. Now I was worried he was too scared! Why was it so hard to let him face challenges, in his own time, at his own pace?

FACING YOUR FEARS

Everyone, no matter what age, deals with fear and anxieties. However, children *especially* need to encounter and confront fears and anxiety in order to develop resilience, which as we just learned is a key component for handling the difficulties of life.

Some kids will be fearless and frankly, will need to be *taught* some healthy fear. Take my friend Anne. Her kids once flew the coop as tots — the three-year-old leading the eighteen-month-old on a neighborhood adventure while Anne was in the bathroom, of all things! She discovered the front door wide open and raced down the block to find her children playing in the ditch at the end of their street. And the way she tells it, if they weren't afraid of seeking adventure on their own that day, they certainly were ever after! We moms want our kids to be fearless, but we also want them to be smart, and not so impetuous as to ignore wisdom and be *blindly* brave. And it's worth noting that Anne and her husband installed deadbolts on every door in the house shortly after their children went traveling, just in case the lesson didn't stick.

As a mom, you know fear about certain things can be healthy for your child. For instance, you want your child to have a healthy fear of fire and not play with matches. You want your child to know it's not safe to engage with a stranger when you are not around. But you also want them to have a childlike sense of adventure and not see danger around every corner, to run and play with abandon, with worry and fear the farthest thing from their minds. I've often wondered, what's the right balance?

It's hard as a mom to let your child walk home from school alone for the first time, even if you know the neighborhood is safe. It's hard as a mom to watch your daredevil son fly down the black diamond ski hill, even if he's been skiing for years. Sometimes moms just have to bite their lips, chew on their nails, and trust their child to the protection of God.

On the other hand, it's also hard as a mom to watch your child face fear, especially when you know there's nothing to really be afraid of. Young children can be afraid of everything from the dark to the dentist. Isn't it interesting to note that as adults, we still face some of these same fears? It's unsettling to be in complete darkness when you can't even see your hand in front of your face. Snakes give me the creeps and make me want to run from the room screaming. Situations where we are expected to perform make the knees of many grown adults quake (the number one identified adult fear is speaking in public), and I hate to admit it but I avoid the dentist like a plague. We know fear can be healthy and facing it helps all of us be able to handle life, but how do we help our young child face their fears in a healthy way?

We should start with understanding why children are afraid in the first place. While adults may have some of the same fears as their children, young children don't think like adults. They don't have the reasoning skills to decide what's okay and what's scary. Young children also have vivid imaginations, which can result in fearful fantasies. Sometimes what they imagine is scarier than what really is, and they can't always tell the difference. But not all children will fear the same things. Mike, at age two, was *terrified* of clowns, but my daughter at the same age thought they were hilarious.

When your children are fearless and it's *you* who are afraid — waiting for the limb to crack when your child steps out onto it, for her outgoing bravery in a social situation to backfire, you may be so caught up in the oh-no-what-ifs that you miss the moment: His first time leaping from the high dive — or her success building new friendships in Girl Scouts, despite the risk of rejection.

It's important not to overprotect or overreact, but to help your child assess the situation and face what scares them (or if not them, you!). Let's look at some helpful strategies.

It's okay to talk about it.

Just as we encourage you to put a name to your fear and say it out loud, it's helpful to encourage your child to do the same. By admitting to your child in appropriate ways that you experience fear too, it sends the message, *It's all right to be afraid, and it's good to share your fears and ask for help.* Share what you have learned about a fear they are dealing with, such as going to the dentist. *I don't like going to the dentist either. The noises can be scary, but I remind myself that the dentist is my friend who wants to help me have healthy teeth.* (I really do remind myself of this when I have to get my teeth cleaned!)

I wish I would have learned earlier to not say to my kids, *Big boys (or girls) don't get scared.* Hopefully we've clearly established in this book that of course they do, and that's okay! Making our children feel shame about their fear only pushes it underground where it can grow and fester. And we know as moms that keeping our fears secret only makes them bigger in our minds. In fact, sometimes you could even admit to your kids that you fear for their safety or welfare — but not as a way to control them or make them fearful. Instead, you admit it to show them your love for them and your trust in your Father who protects them. Sometimes you can even come to agreement on a plan that will help them spread their wings, and help you be less fearful — like a phone call when they arrive at their destination, or a reasonable curfew they need to honor.

What if your *kids* are bold and courageous, but *you* are waiting in the wings for your son to flub his line in the school play, or your daughter to tumble off the climbing wall she dared to attempt? As moms, we all have hold-your-breath moments when our children are taking a risk — whether they are tackling a school play or the world's tallest jungle gym. The key is to ask yourself, *Am I afraid because my child is too brave, or because I'm worried they might fail?* Eight-year-olds have no business climbing around on the roof of your house, but they can and should heartily attack the playground equipment at your neighborhood

HELPING YOUR CHILD BE BRAVE

park. And if your sometimes shy child volunteers to give a presentation in class, or tries out for the school play—applaud his efforts to push through shyness to shine in a new way. Failure on the playground or in front of the class can be painful (*What if she breaks her arm? What if he freezes during his speech? What if…*) but this is how learning happens. When we let them fail, we let them grow. This is the stuff motherhood is made of.

Send a fearless message.

Do fear and anxiety creep into your language? I began to think long and hard about this when I noticed a particular phrase coming out of my mouth in almost every conversation with my kids. *Be careful.* I found myself saying it at the pool, at the park, as my kids headed out the back door to play. It became a standard closing to my conversations, like Walter Cronkite's signature signoff on the CBS evening news, "And that's the way it is." Really? Did I really want my kids to remember their mom always admonishing them to be careful, like a tag-along warning to have a little bit of fun, but not too much, because it was more important to be safe?

I began to listen to myself carefully in conversations. Why did I feel the need to add those words at every turn? Sure, I wanted to educate my kids on proper precautions and talk to them about dangerous risks and being sensible, but I was already doing that. It was as if I was trying to control the amount of danger with my words, *be careful.* I still catch myself doing this, even with my adult children as they head out the door with their car keys. I hesitate to admit it, but I caught myself saying it to the guy who sacked my groceries and helped me take them to the car. "Oh, be careful, watch your fingers," came out of my mouth as he shut the car door. He just smiled.

Help your child manage their fear by making sure you are managing yours. Replace your worrisome words with words of joy. I'm reminding myself daily to replace my "be careful" with "have fun!" Life *is* fun, and the message I want to send to my kids is to go for it!

Model being unfearful.

It's true that our children watch us every day and we are their biggest role models, not just in behavior but in how they approach life. Your child takes their cues from you when it comes to meeting new people and encountering new things and experiences. Many children become fearful of spiders or bugs because they see us freaking out when a bee buzzes by their head. Notice the times when your child is afraid (like during a thunderstorm), and seize the opportunity to model, "This is what I do when I face something scary." Try singing or turn on some music and dance away the thunder noise.

I was once in a classroom of kindergartners and the lights went out during a storm. This can be a scary moment for a young child, but the wise teacher immediately called out, "Surprise! You didn't know the lights were going to go out, did you?" The children laughed.

As our children get older, it's even more important to make

sure that their fear (or ours!) doesn't keep them from missing out on what life has to offer them. Again, I think we can be powerful models for our kids. Does fear keep you from stepping into a new opportunity? Does the fact that you can't predict how everything will turn out stop you from taking a risk? As I've talked with moms who want to grow in not only overcoming their fears but modeling brave choices for their kids, I've been inspired by their bold moves. Sarah shares her story of an unusual opportunity and what caused her to jump in.

What Could Brave Look Like? Sarah's Story

My children were three and five when my husband asked me a question that would challenge my trust in God more than anything else ever has.

"Want to get a sailboat and sail around the world?"

"What?"

At the time, we lived in landlocked Colorado and I'd never sailed any kind of boat in my life! Was he joking? Immediately I laughed it off, but when Mark didn't laugh along with me I realized he was completely serious. As I listened to him excitedly tell me of his childhood dreams to sail, my mind raced with questions and fears. How would I feed my family? How could I protect my children and make sure all their needs were met? Could I handle living in such a tight space with my family without going nuts? Then scenes from *Jaws, The Perfect Storm,* and *Castaway* started popping into my head. I envisioned huge waves crashing over the bow and the kids huddled below, wet and shivering. I was afraid of the unknown, the uncomfortable, and the unexpected. I was terrified, but Mark was *thrilled.* He shared how he felt God was calling our family to a very unusual ministry opportunity, if we would just go out and meet people that we might never meet any other way.

I began to pray and search for God's guidance in spite of my anxieties. What was his plan for us? I read in Psalms 139:7–10 that even if I "make my bed in the depths," God's hand would lead me and hold me. I reminded myself of 2 Timothy 1:7 where it says God didn't give us a spirit of fear, but of power and love and self-control. I decided to focus on the blessings that God had in store for us, rather than the "what ifs." I became excited about the time we'd get to spend together, learning and exploring. My questions turned from fear to anticipation. What would we see? Who would we meet? How would this change us? What would my kids experience that they couldn't at home?

As a mom, I had always tried to control my surroundings and create an environment of comfort and familiarity for my family. I made weekly menus, taxied the kids around from one activity to another, and scheduled playdates, library visits, and teeth cleanings. I was a creature of habit, safe and secure in my tiny predictable corner of the world. I began to ask myself the question, *But did I really need God or rely on him?* I also wanted my kids to see me not backing down from an opportunity out of fear. I didn't want to hide my fear from my kids, but I wanted to model what trust in God really was. It's stepping out when you don't know how everything will work out. It's holding his hand instead of having all the answers. It's jumping into out-of-the-ordinary ministry opportunities that don't always make sense to others.

We did go on that adventure. We have lived aboard for two years now, and that predictable world I once knew is long gone. Today, we drive our dinghy to a dock, find the local market, pick out whatever foods look freshest, and carry them all back to figure out dinner. No place is familiar, I can't make pre-planned menus, and there are very few playdates. But God is with us. We see him in the blanket of stars on our night sails, in joyful faces of the local children we play with on the beaches, in jubilant hymns sung in windowless churches, in wondrous creatures underwater and flying above, and in our family's growing relationships. I wouldn't have experienced any of this had I let my fears keep me where I was. I have learned that fears are powerless and often meaningless once you decide to turn them over to our great big God and say "yes." 🌸

I WANT TO SEE YOU BE BRAVE

For most of us, we will never have the opportunity to go on a sailing adventure like Sarah's, but perhaps you have other opportunities in your life that seem too big and scary to pursue. Could God be asking you to step into a new calling that seems too big to tackle? Are there opportunities or adventures that have caused you to look the other way because you can't figure out all the "what ifs"? If you feel a tug on your heart as you read this, God may be calling your name.

Moms, here's where I am, and it's taken me a long time to get here. I want to model a healthy relationship with fear for my kids, not a "danger around every corner" mentality. I want to be available and ready if God calls me to something dangerous. I want to model a robust sense of adventure and a "zest for life" attitude for my kids to see, through pursuing what I love and being willing to take risks. It hasn't been easy, because as I stated in chapter one, I'm no rookie when it comes to fear and worry. It's been a part of me my entire life and lifetime habits are hard to break. I can't do it on my own, but I'm learning to tap into some powerful spiritual rhythms.

Spiritual Rhythms
for the Everyday Mama

I'm no spiritual giant. Days go by without my taking time to pray. I'm terrible at memorizing Scripture and I have to write my verses on index cards and read them a million times before they sink in. I get caught up with me, myself, and I in my prayer time, to the point that I wonder if I'm boring God to tears. I find myself getting terribly bossy with God. *God, why aren't you taking my fear away? God, are you even listening?* I forget to be thankful. But still I know he loves me. He's there to help me in my mom fear. He wants me to be brave and he wants to help me raise brave kids. For me, it's a continuous journey in facing my mom fears, but I'm learning some practices that help even an everyday mama like me.

Pray big.

In chapter six, I mentioned I no longer pray for God to keep my kids safe. This was quite a turn for me and I still find myself sliding back into my fear-based prayers. *Oh God, don't let Brittainy get in an accident. Lord, keep Mike and Hilary and the girls from harm.* It's not that I don't want them safe. Of course I do. But my God is bigger than this. He created them to do big audacious things, scary things that make Satan want to run the other way. This is what I want for my kids. I want God to make them dangerous, to use them in ways they haven't even dreamed of yet. I want him to blow their minds with what he can accomplish through them. And I want to be the kind of mom who is not afraid when it happens.

But here's a mistake I've made in praying this way. I kept it a secret. I was asking God to make my kids dangerous but I wasn't telling them. Now I share it with them because I want them to know I'm *praying* for them to be brave. And I also want them to know I'm asking God to give me a brave mom heart to go with it.

Speak God's Word over your kids.

Mom — your words are powerful. And did you know that you can speak life *to* your kids and *over* your kids? Proverbs 18:21 tells us that our tongue has the power of life and death. Clearly our words matter and what we pray makes a difference. When you choose to speak the Word of God over your children, you are choosing to speak God's promises of life and blessing over them. I have found this to be a powerful tool in my prayer life to help me pray courageously for my kids. Here are some of my favorites, reworded slightly to refer more directly to my children:

My children are blessed and will be mighty in the land. (Psalm 112:2)

My children will fulfill God's will and purpose for their lives. (Psalm 138:8)

My children are children in whom there is no blemish. They are well favored. They are skillful in wisdom, cunning in knowledge, and understand science. They have the ability to stand in the king's palace and teach others. (Daniel 1:4)

My children are not being conformed to this world's system, but they are constantly being transformed by the renewing of their mind, that they might know what is the good, acceptable, and perfect will of God for their lives. (Romans 12:2)

My children will flee from all sexual immorality and impurity in thought, word, or deed, and they will realize that their body is the temple of the Holy Spirit. (1 Corinthians 6:18 – 19)

My children are examples to others in life, in love, in faith, and in purity. (1 Timothy 4:12)

Prayer is a mighty tool, and the verses above are just a few of God's promises of blessing and power. As moms, we have the right to ask God to make them true for our children.

Steep your mind in truth.

I'm normally a coffee girl, but every once in a while I love a cup of hot, stout tea. However, the tea bag has to have the proper amount of time to steep in the cup. If I pull it out too quick, the tea is weak and bland. The same is true for us as moms. When we haven't spent enough time soaking in truth, we find ourselves weak and ineffective. It's true that you will never be a perfect mom. It's true that you will face fears throughout your life. It's also true that your children will too. But here are some powerful truths to let your mind steep in:

> God's got your back as a mom. He gave you the children you have, and he has a great plan for you as a brave mom who raises brave kids. (Jeremiah 29:11)

> God not only loves you but he thinks about you. He delights in you. He's proud of you. (Zephaniah 3:17)

> No matter how you fail as a mom, or how many mistakes you make, God is there for you. (1 John 1:9)

> God dreams big and he wants us to too. (Ephesians 3:20)

> God knows we have fear and we worry but he's ready to help. (Philippians 4:6)

When you let your mind settle into these truths, it's hard for fear to be in control. Truth busts fear and leaves it powerless. Truth brings fear into the light, where it looks small and very manageable. But just saying these truths isn't enough. Spend time thinking about what they could really mean for your life. Let them settle in as you steep in their power.

When we started this journey together, we asked you if you could picture yourself as a brave mom. Can you see it? It's you, knowing you are not alone in your fear. It's you, wearing a tool belt full of truths that you can brandish when panic strikes and armed with strategies that build your peaceful and confident heart. It's you, walking in confidence because you know fear has no power over you. You are a brave mom facing her real-mom fears.

A Closing Prayer

Dear God, as moms we come before you acknowledging that this job is too big for us to do on our own. We need you. Please give us the courage to be the mom you called us to be, as we give our fears over to you. Help us to dream big. Help us to remember that you gave us the children we have and that you have equipped us completely to be the best mom that our children could ever need or want. We need not fear because you are with us.

LET'S GET PRACTICAL

1. In what ways do you see your child struggling with fear? Or in what ways has their fearlessness struck fear in *your* heart?

2. Do you have a spiritual rhythm or practice that helps you in being brave or helps you in developing a brave child? What is it? Have you shared it with another mom?

3. What are the top three takeaways or ways you have grown from reading this book?

Share your takeaways or ways you want to continue to grow in being a brave mom with your spouse, a friend, or a mentor. Ask them to help hold you accountable to continue to grow.

NOTES

1. "Anxiety Disorders: Introduction." www.nimh.nih.gov/health/publications/anxiety-disorders/index.shtml. Accessed May 5, 2014.

2. "Fear/Phobia Statistics." www.statisticbrain.com/fear-phobia-statistics. Accessed May 5, 2014.

3. Lissa Rankin, "How Fear Makes You Sick." (Posted January 31, 2013), www.lissarankin.com/how-fear-makes-you-sick. Accessed April 7, 2014.

4. Ibid.

5. Connie Matthiessen, "Top 5 Parenting Fears and What You Can Do About Them." www.babycenter.com/0_top-5-parenting-fears-and-what-you-can-do-about-them_3656609.bc. Accessed April 8, 2014.

6. Ibid.

7. Ibid.

8. Ibid.

9. David Finkelhor, "Fives Myths About Missing Children." (Posted May 10, 2013), www.washingtonpost.com/opinions. Accessed April 8, 2014.

10. Benjamin Radford, "Child Abductions by Strangers Very Rare." (Posted May 14, 2013), www.news.discovery.com. Accessed April 8, 2014.

11. Gavin De Becker, *Protecting the Gift: Keeping Children and Teenagers Safe (And Parents Sane)* (New York: Dell Publishing, 1999), 187.

12. Matthiessen, "Top 5 Parenting Fears."

13. Shaun Dreisbach, "Top 14 Pregnancy Fears (And Why You Shouldn't Worry)." www.parents.com/pregnancy/complications/health-and-safety-issues/top-pregnancy-fears/#page=5. Accessed April 9, 2014.

14. Kara Powell, *Sticky Faith: Ideas to Build Lasting Faith in Your Kids* (Grand Rapids: Zondervan, 2011), 13.

15. "Evangelism Is Most Effective Among Kids." (Posted October 11, 2004), www.barna.org/barna-update/article/5-barna-update/196-evangelism-is -most-effective-among-kids#.Uw4yZM6hb2Y. Accessed April 9, 2014.

16. Diana Landon, "10 Things I Love about My Teen." www.momlogic.com. Accessed 2010. Resource is no longer available online.

17. Aparna Mathur, Hao Fu, and Peter Hansen, "The Mysterious and Alarming Rise of Single Parenthood in America." (Posted September 3, 2013), *www. theatlantic.com/business/archive/2013/09/the-mysterious-and-alarming-rise -of-single-parenthood-in-america/279203/*. Accessed April 9, 2014.